"Faulkner's *Illustrated Guide Adult Edition* is a tool I wish teenager. It would have saved me a lot of financial headaches as I went into college and beyond. This guide contains great tips for adolescents to gain a step-up in winning the Money Game as they enter adulthood. The illustrations, anecdotes, "Cheat Codes," and online games are great additions to Faulkner's guide that young adults are sure to love and learn from."

— **Lana Lunsford, high school teacher and parent**

"As an adjunct faculty member, I can say the majority of new college students today lack the basic financial knowledge they require for both college and life success. This book can change all of this. With excellent teaching methodology, easy to understand text, explanatory stories, and a variety of illustrations — this book aces teaching financial concepts and skills."

— **Karen Basso, adjunct college professor**

"I am buying a copy for all my grandkids and telling them how important this book will be to their future."

— **Billy Ring, grandparent**

"I wish this book would've been around when I was in high school. It would have saved me a lot of problems. I definitely plan on having my teenagers read this book. It is full of information they desperately need to know."

— **Carla Urbanas: small business owner and parent**

"This book explains how school loans work in real life. I also enjoyed the business concepts, and the inner workings of cryptocurrency, the stock market, and investments."

— **Lily Malott, high school student**

"This is the only financial book I have read in my life, and I am so glad it was this book! It was easy to read and understand. I particularly loved the stories of amazing financial success achieved by dozens of high school and college students."

— **Lauren Pimentel, college student**

"This book is a great resource for middle school to college-aged people who want to learn critical, real-life financial literacy skills that schools don't teach. It's a quick and easy read and can teach anyone how to budget, manage money, invest and let time do the rest."

— Jennifer Tung, payments lawyer

"Wow! Larry has hit a home run with his latest book. As a thirty-year veteran high school teacher and professional speaker, this book hits the mark with easy-to-understand language and great illustrations. This is a must read for all young adults who wish to have a positive and secure financial future. Larry takes you there with ease step by step. Well done my friend."

— Dave Leedy, high school teacher, youth leader, parent

"In *The Illustrated Guide to Financial Independence: Young Adult Edition*, Larry Faulkner takes what could be considered dense material and re-imagines it into a relatable format that makes learning the steps to financial freedom interesting and accessible for the teen audience. The modern real-world examples, step-by-step guides, practical budgeting advice, attainable goal-setting, and fantastic illustrations all come together to create a valuable resource for young adults who are interested in understanding financial literacy but don't know where to begin. I plan on adding a copy to the Young Adult collection at the library where I work, and I'll be purchasing a copy for my own teen; the book is that great."

— Anna Dussler, young adult library collection developer

"*The Illustrated Guide to Financial Independence: Young Adult Edition* empowers its readers with the knowledge they need to make informed decisions and achieve financial independence. A must-read for anyone serious about mastering their finances."

— Monnie Bush, Founder and CEO of Victory Project, an after school mentoring project for 8th to 12th graders.

The Illustrated Guide to
FINANCIAL INDEPENDENCE
YOUNG ADULT EDITION

LARRY FAULKNER

Illustrations by Douglas Brown

Published by
Faulkner Financial Freedom

ISBN: 979-88604230-5-3

Cover designed by Douglas Brown, albumartist.com
Interior designed by Danielle H. Acee, authorsassistant.com

Special thanks to Danielle Hartman Acee and her crackerjack team at authorsassistant.com. As I often say, "Nothing happens without Danielle."

This book is dedicated to
my three wonderful sons who each created
their own financially independent lives.
I am so proud to be your dad!

Table of Contents:

"Wealth flows from energy and ideas."
— **William Feather**

Introduction

Why This Book Is Worthy of Your Valuable Time

Around nine years of age, our oldest son convinced one of his brothers to help him with a business idea. The two began their own business by loading their red wagon with snacks and a cooler filled with bottled water, soda, and other drinks. The boys pulled the wagon down the street to where they were constructing new homes. They resold the inventory in their wagon to the construction workers for a large profit and even developed routine customers. The boys also catered their inventory to meet the requests of their customers for specific snacks and drinks to create more sales.

Eventually, the homes were all built, and this market dried up. Undeterred, my eldest's next business was walking the neighborhood dogs daily. In return, the dogs' owners paid him for his time. He worked on this business for a while, and then tried a lawn work business. He wasn't really thrilled with either of those ventures because of the large time commitment and effort relative to his return of income, although at that age he had trouble expressing it in those terms.

A year later, his next venture was becoming our community paper delivery boy. He minimized his time spent on delivery by using rollerblades to speed up his route time (this was back in the '90s). This method was faster than using a bicycle because he did not have to get on and off his bike. He learned to go up and down steps on rollerblades and he could jump off the neighbors' porches with ease. His skills on the blades became the envy of all the young kids in the neighborhood.

He was also an early adopter of computer technology. He loved computers and spent time reading and learning about them whenever he could. At age 12, he decided he wanted to build his own computer. I spent a lot of time trying to dissuade him from his plan and explained why it would be a bad idea. He ignored my advice and did it anyway. He bought the parts and put them together himself…and proved me entirely wrong. This was long before the "plug and play" of today, so almost every component required some type of programming to work. I had no idea how to do any of these things, but somehow, he did.

When he was thirteen years old, he wanted to take some college courses on computers and the internet that he'd found at our local community college. I took him, but he was disappointed to find that he already knew more than the course taught. After completing a couple of classes, he lost interest because he wasn't learning anything new. Instead, he began taking adult-level computer coding classes and other technology-related certification courses.

Long before he could drive, my son was building websites for individuals and small businesses for cash—sometimes free for charities. This was back in the days when websites had to be built by code. By the time he reached high school, he had certifications to build networks and computer systems. Once he could drive, he built a thriving and profitable computer training and repair business which raked in more money (especially from older clientele) than I would have ever believed possible. The thought of getting a "regular" job never really appealed to him. He did have one briefly but didn't like the restrictions on his time.

His high school teachers and staff soon discovered that he had a high degree of technical ability, which led to them using him extensively for IT work, since the school district's IT department was not very responsive to the school staff. I am not sure how many of his high school classes he actually attended as he seemed to spend a lot his time completing computer tasks for each of his teachers. His work at the high school soon led to even more private contracts, many with local businesses, and an increase in after school income opportunities.

Immediately after graduation, however, he had some bumps in the road. He had obtained a credit card to buy equipment and learned that he had created more debt than he could easily pay because he spent the money he earned instead of paying his bills. This caused him a lot of aggravation and took time and work to dig out of the hole he created. This was very painful for him and taught him a lesson he still remembers to this day.

Today, our son runs the network (construction division) of one of the largest technology companies in the world. He has never taken more than six formal college classes in his life, yet he performs at the cutting edge of network construction technology and leads a large and talented team. Although he does not have a lot of formal college education, he has hundreds of hours invested in the area of self-directed education.

He is now paid extremely well for his self-developed talents and abilities. He has also learned to invest by buying assets and holding them for his family's future, all while studiously avoiding debt—a skill he learned from his experience. Today, he is very focused on building his family's net worth and wants to become financially independent.

He never worries much about losing his job or getting laid off. My son is confident he could have a business up and running on his own, have another job in just a few days or simply be okay with no job at all if he had to take a break for a while, because he has the financial resources to do so.

This story has some very consequential lessons:

1. Right after high school graduation, you will be forced to play the Money Game whether you want to play or not. What you do early in your Money Game really matters. You must play this game for the rest of your life; you cannot quit. It won't matter that you were taught next to nothing about money. You will be expected to jump into the game with both feet. To win this game, you will need to learn important principles that will make the difference between success or eking out a meager existence.

2. At the most basic level, to win (build financial prosperity), you need only perform a few essential tasks: earn money, save your money, and invest your money. That's it! These three simple tasks fuel the entire prosperity-building process.

3. A consumer-driven existence will put you into debt slavery. This is a deadly trap in the Money Game that will damage your chances of financial success. Being in significant debt is a difficult and stressful existence, even if the debt you created was needed to further your education.

Additionally, debt can create poor physical and mental health outcomes due to the high level of stress it generates.

4. Believing you can do something very likely means that you can actually do it—even if you are only ten years old.

5. A formal education does not assure your future success. What will ensure your success is having skills that are in high demand. Become skilled at something so important, people are willing to wait in line for a chance that you might help them or do whatever it takes to employ you. Such skills only come from relentless self-development. Sure, part of it can come from formal education, but formal education alone will not enable you to succeed in today's world.

6. Perceptions and thinking control amazing chunks of our lives—not just our financial world but all aspects of our lives. Financial opportunities are all around us, all of the time. They are so abundant that it may be hard to choose only one. The problem is, we are usually blind to most of them. We stumble and trip over these opportunities every day walking down our chosen path. Instead of recognizing them for what they are, we curse them for getting in our way and holding up our progress. The good news is, when we begin recognizing a few financial opportunities, the others become easier to spot. It is a skill like any other and you can develop it. This principle is equally important in many other facets of your life. For example, if you are looking for reasons the world is unfair and your life stinks, that is what you will easily find. It is vitally important to be very careful what you seek in life. You will very likely find it.

1

Create Economic Momentum

"People who succeed have momentum. The more they succeed, the more they want to succeed, and the more they find a way to succeed." — **Tony Robbins**

Tony Robbins understands forward momentum. He began his own journey by becoming an entrepreneur, then a bestselling author, then a philanthropist, a business strategist and then an extremely gifted motivational speaker. Robbins believes the hardest part in any endeavor is just getting started. Once you are up and running it creates a type of forward motion that builds upon itself. He likens momentum to a rocket that utilizes most of its power to get off the launch pad. Once it gets going, the progress becomes faster and easier. Robbins is worth listening to in this area, as he has built a net worth believed to be around $600 million.

Tony Robbins did not start life with money or any family advantages. He was once just another broke kid who had significant family issues. He grew up in Hollywood with a drug addicted mother who was also physically abusive. Robbins, however, became interested in *money early in life because he was always broke. He was only in junior high school when he began studying money and the differences between those who were broke and those who had money. At seventeen, he was out of school and working as a janitor. He was barely surviving financially. Robbins began spending what little extra money he could scrape together going to motivational and marketing seminars. He also discovered he had a talent for public speaking. From there, Robbins was off and running with upward financial momentum.*

Back in the days when dinosaurs roamed the earth and there was no such thing as the internet, I was a lowly junior high student. I very much wanted a car as soon as I could possibly get one. My desire for a vehicle was powered by the length of my school bus ride as well as the daily harassment and physical bullying I received at the hands of a small group of kids on the bus. The bullies were a tight-knit group of older kids that lived in a small village located down the road from my house in our farming and suburban community.

Obviously, I needed to get some cash together for a car to make my escape. There were very few jobs or small business opportunities in my neighborhood of farm fields, beyond hiring out as labor to farmers, which I did each fall at harvesting time. Harvesting hay paid well but it was incredibly hard work. Also, these jobs typically lasted only a few days.

I soon found a great summer job about five miles away at a local dog boarding kennel that cared for people's pets when they were on vacation. I loved the job. I really enjoyed working with the dogs and other various pets. I would ride my bike there before and after work each day. What I had not considered was that my bike ride (the only practical road to and from work that was doable on a bicycle) took me past that same small village where my bullies lived. On the best days, I would only receive insults or curses as I rode by them. On other days, it would become more physical.

Since I was highly motivated to escape this situation, I managed to save several thousand dollars over several years of summer and fall work. I bought a car soon after turning sixteen. It was a used, beautifully maintained, canary yellow Chevrolet Nova fastback with black pin striping. It was an absolutely beautiful ride and looked like it was going a 100 mph while sitting in the parking lot at school. My parents were kind enough to pay for my insurance. I was responsible for gas and maintenance of the vehicle.

This got me away from the excruciating school bus ride and away from my tormentors. This made my life much easier. Not only that, but the vehicle also opened up a whole world of mobility— which was no small thing considering I lived miles and miles from nearly everything. I was now able to drive to our local town and obtain better paying jobs.

I do not consider myself a "work really hard to become wealthy" person. The wealthy never focus on working hard, they focus on working smart. The "work hard to earn money" concept is simply a cultural norm that isn't necessarily true—as you will soon see in the stories below. Besides, if working hard was the only requirement for success, then workers such as nurses, construction workers, trash collectors, farmers and a whole lot of other professionals would all be rich. The ability to work hard is always a plus, but more is needed.

The most important point of the above story is that my initial economic success built upon itself. Not only that, but my initial success in setting and achieving this reasonably big goal for a high school student was a major milestone in my life. With this one achievement, I built the self-confidence I needed to create new goals and truly believe I could achieve them.

Around this same time, a book called *How to Win Friends and Influence People* by Dale Carnegie inspired me to believe I could set a goal of becoming a millionaire.[1] The book talked about setting performance goals to create the outcomes—including financial—you need.

Then, at the age of twenty-three, I began my law enforcement career as a municipal police officer. This long-term goal allowed me to help people and at the same provided me with some daily excitement, adventure, and a sense of service to my community. It also provided a pension that would be another income stream and supplement any wealth I created. A book published in 1976, *Sylvia Porter's Money Book: How to Earn It, Spend It, Save It, Invest It, Borrow It, And Use It to Better Your Life,* taught me it wasn't necessarily how much money you made that would make you wealthy, but how much you kept and invested that would allow you to succeed financially.[2]

I immediately began saving money and investing with my first paycheck at the police department. A few years later, I met Lisa (now my wife of over 31 years) at a local hospital emergency room, where she was a nurse. I and several officers brought in a shooting victim for emergency treatment. I was immediately attracted to Lisa and asked her out on a date. Lisa initially refused, saying she didn't like to date police officers. Undeterred, I persisted until she finally gave me a chance. We were married a year later, and we raised three boys together.

Lisa and I were on the same page with our financial goals from the very beginning. We were both true believers in the goal-setting process and immediately set a shared goal of achieving financial independence early in our lives. We had regular meetings on this goal and reviewed our progress. At first, our efforts met with only marginal success; but after reviewing our progress, we began researching and learning more about the subjects of budgeting, saving, and investing. We frequently spent evenings taking turns reading financial books to each other or reading books independently and providing a summary to each other. With each new book we finished, we accomplished another short-term goal.

Additionally, our newly gained knowledge also proved the extra push we needed to re-start our forward momentum. I became a millionaire at age fifty-three, and Lisa was still in her forties. We now have the freedom to live the life we wanted.

One of the ways you keep moving forward successfully is to immediately set new goals after reaching the objective(s) you achieved. Reaching a goal provides you with positive emotions and a sense of satisfaction that is very valuable for conquering new goals.[3] If you don't keep your momentum moving forward, it will stall, and you could become stuck in a cycle of working hard but achieving no real financial progress.

I am not the only one who capitalized on forward momentum to maximize success. Others have learned to do this as well. Below is a list of seven teens who created their own opportunities consistent with their interests and passions. These teens used their initial economic success in the Money Game to grow into even better opportunities.

Teen Multi-Millionaire High School Students Who Still Continue to Grow:

1. **Charli D'Amelio:** At the age of seventeen, Charli started making TikTok videos. She is now the world's highest paid TikTok influencer, a TV personality, and a legitimate celebrity. She is heavily invested in a clothing line and owns a large portion (stock shares) of several other

clothing companies. She created a stuffed animal merchandising line that is spinning off into an animated series to promote her products.

2. **Jimmy Donaldson, aka MrBeast:** I admit to being a big fan of this young man and his engaging personality. He always knew what he wanted to do—become a YouTube star. He began making content in high school without much success. He began studying the YouTube algorithm to determine what type of content would create the most views. At the insistence of his mother, he tried college right after high school. He quit after only two weeks to return to YouTube content creation. His mother threw him out at 18 in an attempt to motivate him. He eventually began doing stunts on YouTube, which earned him a lot of views. This eventually progressed to philanthropic stunts, and he has filmed himself giving away millions of dollars to deserving people. This content has earned him the status as the most viewed YouTube content creator in history.

3. **Nyla Hayes:** At age thirteen, Nyla began creating and selling her artwork as NFTs—an uncopiable electronic file identifier—that made her a multimillionaire. She has now expanded into other digital art endeavors and partners with several multi-media companies.

4. **Emil Motycka:** At only nine years old, Emil started a lawn mowing business. He enjoyed mowing lawns and created a rapidly growing business. Emil took out a loan for $8,000 when he was only thirteen years old to purchase a commercial lawn mower. This expansion ramped up his economic opportunities. Since then, he has formed Motycka Enterprises and is now a multimillionaire lawn care and freight hauling company owner.

5. **Max Hayden:** At the age of sixteen, Max began a reselling business during the pandemic. He bought large blocks of merchandise in going-out-of-inventory sales. He prioritized the purchase of items that people stuck at home might want during the pandemic, such as video games and gaming consoles. He now owns a warehouse and an online bookstore. Max must limit his time in this business endeavor (parental rule) as he is still attending high school. Amazingly, his business now employs other high school students and a full-time bookkeeper.

Each of these high school students thought outside the box and deviated from the standard behaviors and norms of the average teen. They took a chance and believed in themselves. They also maximized the talents, skills, and gifts they possessed to create something of value others sought. Each student also learned important new business skills that will serve them well in their future.

The young adults also made use of forward momentum and kept moving at full speed once they began to create some initial success. A study at the University of Maryland (2016) noted that psychological momentum (PM) is an important factor for future achievement. This study defined PM as a sequential run of success that is critical to future goal attainment and exceptional future performance. PM has also been demonstrated to provide the following benefits for those who achieve it:

- Greater self-confidence
- Higher self-perceived skill levels
- Better internal self-esteem
- Self-efficacy (the belief you can take actions to control outcomes in your life)

Self-efficacy is critical to your mental health and overall life satisfaction, as you will see in the following chapters. Based upon recent research, it is now believed that PM begins as a conscious thought process, but soon becomes part of your automatic behavior or the operating system of your brain.[4]

In my case, I did NOT become a millionaire-plus in high school. Millionaire status and beyond occurred later for me, but my early successes were essential building blocks for self-efficacy construction (self-confidence and a belief I could accomplish my objective). I needed to believe deep inside my soul that I could achieve my millionaire goal.

> There are so many economic opportunities available today that even high school students can become millionaires and even multi-millionaires while they are still in school. This is no exaggeration, as there are literally hundreds of teen multi-millionaires.

If envisioning and then creating your ideal future sounds appealing to you, then the first secret is to just get started and create forward momentum toward your goals. One of the ways you can create that momentum is by learning the financial ins and outs of personal finance, just as my wife Lisa and I did years ago.

> Universal principles: Learning and knowledge are the first vital steps in creating forward momentum. It is also a universal principle that those who do nothing accomplish nothing.

OPPORTUNITY
SOLAR POWER

OPPORTUNITY
RAIN TO GROW CROPS

OPPORTUNITY
SELL FRUIT?

FINANCIAL
OPPORTUNITIES
ARE ALL AROUND
YOU. LEARN TO
RECOGNIZE
THEM.

OPPORTUNITY
SELL VS BUY VS RENT

OPPORTUNITY
SELL FOR USE IN
LANDSCAPING

Cheat Codes:

The most significant concepts covered in this chapter begin with the vital importance of creating economic success in your life. Creating even a small financial success in the present has the potential to build upon itself and create persistent upward economic momentum well into your future. Your continued success can even create a type of psychological momentum (PM) and is an important factor in building the desire and confidence so that you can create the life you want.

Believing that you must work very hard to create income is a cultural view and not necessarily a reality. Working hard is not a requirement if you have the ability to work "smart."

Up Next:

Keep reading to learn about the Money Game you will be playing once you graduate from high school. We must all play this game, whether we want to play it or not. In the next chapter I will explain why it will be so important to commit yourself to winning this game. Sadly, most people do not win the game and later regret their life decisions. I will explain how to avoid that fate and create a life others wish they had.

Online Resources:

Online game: Fistful of Dollars. In this online game you take over the Galactic Zappers Company. You must ensure that the company maintains a steady cash flow to resupply your inventory and make sure items are always available for sale. You can borrow money or take items on credit from suppliers. You can also reject customers if they seem illegitimate. Play the game here: https://sims.myej.org/fistfulofdollars/

Take this online test to determine your type of thinking.
My quiz results said I am an energized thinker. "Energized thinking is at the intersection of 'Big Picture' and 'Actions'. Energizers like to set a bold vision, rally people around a cause, and mobilize resources to achieve an important objective." This is no surprise given my story. Take the quiz here: https://www.causeit.org/what-kind-of-thinker-are-you-quiz

2

Why You Must Win the Money Game

"Many financial problems people face today started when they were young and making their first few financial decisions." — **Vince Shorb, CEO, National Financial Education Council**

ince Shorb was an unusual child. When Vince was in grade school, he was fascinated with learning about the way money worked and how it grew. This gave Shorb a big financial head start in life. When Shorb was twenty years old, he was a real estate investor who owned rental properties, had investments in the stock market, and had already built a successful business. His early decision to learn about money and make building prosperity a priority in his life makes him stand apart from the vast majority of young people who live from paycheck to paycheck.[1]

I was older than Vince Shorb when I began my own financial journey. My interest in money began when I was in high school. I can still remember that I was a junior, sitting in history class, not really paying attention to the lecture. As the teacher taught the day's history lesson, I was mentally engaged in thinking about my life and where it was headed. I was uncomfortable with the negative direction my life seemed to be traveling—fueled entirely by my negative attitude and bad behaviors.

It was at this point I realized that I had many resentments about my life and that my feelings about my family were fueling the negative behaviors I exhibited. My feelings, upon further reflection, were irrelevant and would never help me in the long run. If I wanted to succeed and be happy in my life, it was all up to me. I needed to be successful for me. No one was going to hand me anything. It was on this day that I decided that I wanted to be successful and create a happy life. It was in that class at that time, that I decided I wanted to become a millionaire. I didn't exactly know how to go about it yet, so from that point forward I made it a goal to learn as much as possible.

The success I had saving, purchasing a car at a relatively young age, and the research I completed on my own about money gave me the confidence to believe I had the power to control my financial destiny. These experiences created my inner belief that you don't have to accept the cards you were dealt. You can change everything in your life if you are willing to put forth the effort. This view regarding self-determination allowed me to create positive financial momentum that helped me achieve my financial goal of creating over a million dollars in assets.

If you want to choose your own financial destiny, rather than leaving it to chance, your first step is contained in the sentence below:

The first step on your journey is making an active choice to become financially independent.

**BUILDING
WEALTH IS A MATTER OF
PRIORITIES!**

**IF YOU VALUE THIS OUTCOME,
YOU WILL ADJUST TO
MAKE IT HAPPEN.**

**IF YOU DON'T VALUE IT, THEN IT
WILL NOT HAPPEN.**

Just as both Vince Shorb and I did, you must consciously choose financial independence and make it a priority. If it is not a priority, it simply won't happen. If it is a priority, you will find ways to adjust your behaviors to achieve your goals.

Most Americans do not make the decision to prioritize their financial life outcomes. The primary factor that holds us back from this decision is that most of us are so uneducated about money, we don't understand why we should even bother. Growing up, most people are taught next to nothing about the role of money in our lives, let alone how to build wealth. This lack of knowledge creates consistent, negative consequences throughout life.

Add to this dilemma, when finances are occasionally taught in school, traditional methods are used to teach the lessons. This method of teaching financial literacy can be both extremely boring and ineffective! The result of this substandard approach can create minimal engagement from the student and almost no behavioral change.

For example, consider a lesson about building a budget in which a student is traditionally taught where to get the numbers for their budgets. They are taught about restricting their lifestyle and the chore of recording their spending. Such a lesson would have done absolutely nothing to inspire me to listen to this type of lecture any more than the history lesson I was ignoring when I first set my goal to become financially independent.

Instead, what if someone told me they could teach me to use a budget to create the life of my dreams? What if they said these financial lessons could provide me with most of the things I wanted in life? What if they started each lesson with a true short story that explained the principle in the upcoming financial lesson and how it had improved someone's life? Provide these types of lesson plans and you suddenly would have most students' undivided attention.

I want to avoid the common pitfall of boring you about personal finance, so the format we will use throughout this book is to combine facts and figures, explanations of why a concept is useful to you and then typically add personal stories that explain the concept in a way that you will remember it. Science shows we remember stories a lot easier than we remember facts. Such stories allow our brains to remember concepts, principles and even lists by connecting them to mental images and emotions.[2]

One of our first steps is for us to get on the same page. Since we are going to be using the words financial independence throughout the entire book, let us define the term financial independence. Financial independence is accumulating financial wealth (also known as prosperity in this book) to a point where you no longer require a traditional job to support yourself while you live your chosen lifestyle. Having a comfortable life and being secure in your finances requires much less work than living the lavish lifestyle of a Hollywood celebrity. Both lifestyles are possible, but it all depends on which lifestyle you prefer and how you want to direct your efforts. To calculate how much your ideal lifestyle will cost, use this lifestyle calculator from the Jumpstart Coalition: https://www.jumpstart.org/what-we-do/support-financial-education/reality-check/.[3]

How did it go? Did you feel comfortable with the outcome from the lifestyle calculator exercise? The information about the lifestyle you desire is very relevant even if you are still in high school or even if you are now a few years past graduation. What you may not understand just yet is that immediately after high school you will be thrown into the thick of life's Money Game. What you do in this game determines the lifestyle and outcome you obtain in both the short term and the long term. Most Americans are entirely unprepared to navigate, let alone win, life's Money Game. If you want to choose both your own destiny and financial health, you must very quickly learn how to play this game at a high level.

> unfortunately, being forced to play life's Money Game without adequate training is like playing a video game for the first time and being required to conquer every level and win the game the first time you play it.

According to the Financial Educators Council, the average score on a very basic financial literacy test for young adults, aged 15 to 18 years of age, is a dismal 63% and 19 to 24 years of age is barely competent at 71% on a normal grading scale.[4] This is hardly a score that will help the average high school graduate win the Money Game or choose their own destiny.

Additionally, recent surveys point out that parents have not been a lot of help in preparing you to play the Money Game. The survey shows that most (not all) parents dread teaching their kids about money.[5] Your parents likely don't feel they do that great with money themselves. They certainly do not want to give you bad advice, so it is natural for them to avoid discussing this subject with you. Most parents simply tell their kids to save money, create a budget and don't go into debt to buy stupid stuff. This is all certainly great advice, but you need to know more.

TIP: Don't assume your parents know nothing about money. Asking your parents for money or business lessons might end up paying you big dividends. They might possess experience and knowledge that is extremely valuable to your future. You have no idea what your parents know or don't about money, business, and success if you don't ask them. A great example is the case of Sean Belnick, who was only fourteen when his stepfather (Gary Glazer) helped him start a business with the $500 Sean had managed to save. His stepdad taught him about drop-shipping, which in this case *was using a website to advertise various products—office chairs that had a strong market. Drop-shipping is a business strategy where a person acts strictly as a third-party seller. When the drop-shipper gets an order, they pass it along to the manufacturer who then delivers the product. This makes the seller essentially a retail outlet. Sean was able to set up a commercial website offering 100 different chairs, providing a one-stop shop for a large variety of office chairs. The website almost immediately took off because of the strong, continual demand for office chairs. Sean is now a multi-millionaire and his business bizchair.com is still going strong.*[6]

So, let's begin your Money Game training to make you a top-level player. The first concept you need to know is explained in the sentence below. What you do with this concept will determine if you will ever have the ability to choose your future destiny:

Money Equals Freedom!

AFTER HIGH SCHOOL YOU WILL BE
FORCED TO PLAY THE "MONEY GAME"
WHETHER YOU WANT TO OR NOT!

IT IS LIKE PLAYING A VIDEO GAME FOR
THE FIRST TIME & BEING REQUIRED TO
BEAT ALL LEVELS & WIN THE GAME THE
FIRST TIME YOU PLAY IT.

The more money you have, the more freedom you get! By freedom, I mean we have control over our future. If we have financial resources, we get to decide what we will or won't do in the future—not some employer. We get to decide which jobs we will take or even whether we will work at all.

THE MORE MONEY YOU HAVE, THE
MORE FREEDOM YOU GET!

Creating a better life by increasing your financial prosperity is a valid concept. Studies show the greater your financial resources, the more satisfied with life you become.[7] Financial prosperity allows you to custom build the life you want and experience it fully. For example, my wife and I love to travel. Therefore, we go on several trips a year. We have traveled to many countries in Europe, cruised to Russia, gone on an African safari, and traveled to China. In America, we are trying to visit all the National Parks. When at home, we can volunteer for social causes we care about—usually financial literacy. This is the life we choose, and we love it.

This life is a very different reality from that experienced by most Americans. Most Americans must work as long as they possibly can to pay their bills. They have very little personal choice since their need to create income to pay bills overrides most of their wants or preferences. Once the average person is no longer able to work due to advanced age or health concerns, they live with meager financial means until they die. Additionally, such debt negatively impacts their health and quality of life,[8] which is why financial freedom stemming from your ability to play the Money Game is vitally important to your future.

I have taught the "choose your financial destiny to create life freedom" lesson in many classes and in many places. Sometimes, I get the response that financial education is only for rich people, or this plan is only for smart people. People who make these comments really don't believe they can create financial prosperity in their lives.

I can tell you for sure that successful players in the Money Game are not part of an exclusive club. Financial abundance does not have a restricted membership list. Anyone can get in if they are willing to learn how the Money Game is played and then put in the effort needed to create the level of success they want.

If you believe becoming financially independent is beyond your reach because of your family's financial status, your family's social status or your personal academic history, here is an encouraging fact: People change course in their lives every day and create their own destinies.

As an example, if you are/were not the greatest student in high school, your grades have very little to do with your ability to create prosperity. The fact is that academic achievement is only modestly related to prosperity. For example, our world leaders were rarely the valedictorians of either their high schools or colleges. The same thing is true inside the world's largest companies. Most CEOs did not have the top grade point averages in their high schools or colleges.[9]

One would think earning potential would be linked to those people who get the best grades, go to the best colleges, then get the best jobs. Those people would then earn the most money and they would create the most wealth. However, this concept just doesn't track in real life. Why? We live in a messy world and face new problems every day. To build financial resources in this environment requires consistent focus, work, persistence, determination, and never-ending resilience.[10]

Others remark they come from very troubled families and/ or past and building financial resources is not possible for them. I am here to tell you, that no matter what your past might be, we possess the near magical power to change our behaviors, alter our perspectives and create our own destinies. Some believe, and I agree with them, that the more difficult your past, the more it can motivate you to succeed. You can choose a new path forward and leave a troubled life behind. That's what I did, and you can do it as well.

For example, take the case of Danny Trejo. He started smoking marijuana when he was only eight years of age. By age twelve, he was addicted to heroin (his uncle helped him shoot up the first time) and ran the streets of Los Angeles to acquire the drugs he craved. This behavior landed him in and out of juvenile detention facilities throughout his teens. As a young adult, Trejo became an armed robber to support his drug habit. His violent behavior landed him in various California prisons. Trejo was once reported to have said he had been inside every prison within the Californian penal system.

Inside prison, Trejo continued his violent behavior. He began boxing and became the welterweight boxing champion of the California prison system. Although this was a positive outlet for him, and made him quite a celebrity inside prison, he used his celebrity status to start a protection racket to make money. Newer inmates had to pay him a stipend or suffer his wrath. He also continued his drug use while in prison.

His behavior finally reached a crisis point when he was thrown into solitary confinement for assaulting a guard with a rock during a prison riot. After a time in solitary, he realized he had to turn his life around. When he was released from solitary confinement, he began a 12-step program while still in prison that allowed him to get sober.

When paroled a few months later, Trejo continued to work the 12-step program by helping others with drug problems stay sober. He was once on a film set helping an actor maintain his sobriety when he got his first big break, and a director grabbed him and used him as an extra to fill a bad guy role. After that, Trejo was off and running acting in films. Trejo is now a multi-millionaire. As Trejo continued to work the 12-step program he learned the joy and value of helping others rather than harming or extorting them. In fact, he has said that the only thing of any worth that has ever happened to him occurred when he was in the process of helping other people.

Trejo used his financial momentum and resources from acting and began his own businesses (such as Trejo's Tacos) and invests in other people's businesses. In short, Trejo has gone from being a prisoner to a becoming a very successful entrepreneur. [11]

Even if you have a troubled past like Danny Trejo, or a terrible academic history in high school like me, you can still build prosperity using simple, mainstream financial concepts that absolutely work! The only caveat is you must make building prosperity an active choice and make that choice one of your priorities. If it is not a priority in your life, it will never happen.

One final point to wrap this chapter up: Sometimes, due to our upbringing, religion or society's message to us, we get the impression that money is evil. I don't believe that is true. Money is an inanimate object like a car. What you can do with a car certainly might be evil—driving recklessly, driving drunk, assault with a vehicle—but the car itself is not. Others believe being wealthy is not fair because of the many poor people in the world. I get that point, but if you want to help the poor, how does being poor yourself help them in any way? Helping the impoverished obtain adequate financial resources or a means of supporting themselves is much more useful to them.

As an example of helping others (other than the money we donate to charities), my wife and I teach financial literacy in prisons and housing projects and to various other groups that request us, and we usually do it for free. We have taught in locations that were soul-crushingly poor. It's not easy to see and just when we wonder if any of our efforts matter, we hear from someone who tells us we made a difference in their life. Also, being financially independent makes it so much easier to provide financial literacy training.

Cheat Codes:

To win the Money Game, you must choose financial prosperity. It will not happen by accident. It is worth the effort to make that choice because money buys freedom; freedom that provides you with increased control over your life. Financial prosperity also typically leads to greater life satisfaction. A lack of financial resources will likely bring hardship and restricted freedom of choice. Having a troubled past does not exclude you from achieving high-level financial goals once you decide to actively choose this outcome. I did it and you can do it as well. Money is just a tool and is neither good nor bad. What matters is what you do with your money.

Up Next:

What kind of person are you? I certainly hope you aren't the kind of person who must learn every lesson the hard way. Experience is a very cruel and unforgiving teacher! Keep reading to learn how to avoid the fate of the uninformed.

Online Resources:

Check out this great online game to boost your financial literacy through career and earnings simulations. Those who play this game report that it was interesting and entertaining: http://finances101thegame.org/wp/online-game/

Want to know where you stand in the area of financial knowledge? Take the financial literacy test here: https://www.finra.org/financial_literacy_quiz

3

Learning Is Much Cheaper Than Experience

"Hard-headed people have to learn things the hard way!"
— **Karen Basso**

Karen Basso is an Occupational Safety and Health Administration (OSHA) safety trainer. She provides education to workers to keep them safe during their workday. Sometimes, during her training sessions, she gets push-back from workers (or employers) who don't want to do the things the rules require. She tries to work with them, but at some point, she ends the conversation with, "Hard-headed people have to learn things the hard way." The phrase does seem to get the attention of people who stubbornly refuse to respond to her OSHA safety training.

Basso enjoys telling a story where employees were working on a wall while standing on scaffolding that seemed wobbly and unstable. The OSHA consultant on the scene told the employer that his employees should have specialized ladder training. The employer said, "We don't have time for that." As if on cue, one of his employees fell off the scaffolding and broke his leg. This ultimately resulted in numerous workers compensation hearings, lost time on the job and extensive paid sick leave for the employee's recovery. This was a very expensive lesson that was learned the hard way by this stubborn employer.

NFL star Brandon Copeland of the NY Jets has a very different mindset than most professional football players. It all started back in high school when Brandon developed a keen interest in both football and money. While still in high school, he interned at a hedge fund and then went on to work at investment companies while attending college. Brandon says he views himself as a corporation whose job it is to make money. This clear mindset has enabled him to invest 60% of his salary every paycheck, save 30% of his salary, while spending only 10% of each paycheck for daily expenses.

Brandon recognizes the troubling trend of four out of five of his teammates going bankrupt or experiencing financial distress after they stop playing pro football. To counteract this trend, Brandon tries to encourage the younger players (around twenty one years old) to begin investing and saving right away. Some players listen to his advice while others must learn these lessons the hard way.[1]

Your lack of experience in the Money Game is currently your biggest obstacle to becoming a top player. If you want to become a higher-level player, you need to minimize the time you spend learning money lessons through experience. As an example, I once purchased an aftermarket warranty on a car I owned. The policy was very expensive, and I soon discovered it covered very little in the way of vehicle repairs. A little research by me before I made this purchase would have easily saved me thousands of dollars in wasted money.

Learning financial lessons through experience is expensive and unfortunately the norm in American society. You are young and can always overcome your past mistakes. I certainly did, but a better path is to gain knowledge through reading and directed study to avoid expensive experience.

When people become older, they desperately wish they could play the Money Game over and do things much better the second time around. A good way to avoid the typical financial mistakes is to learn about the most common mistakes others have made and stay clear of them.

For example, in survey after survey, most elderly Americans list one or more financial errors as one of their top life regrets.[2] A full 80% of all older Americans have at least one significant financial life regret—some have many more.[3]

These regrets are not surprising as money is rated as the number one stressor in modern life.[4] The top life regret related to finances is failing to save enough money—whether the problem is saving enough money for emergencies, not saving enough to invest, or failing to save any money at all.[5] This is a critical problem for half of all Americans. Without the availability of savings, your options to handle life's emergencies narrow and minor problems can escalate into bigger problems. Nearly half of all Americans can't even come up with an extra $400 to pay an unexpected bill.[6] Your life can be much more satisfying with a large savings account balance.

The next most common regret is accumulating too much debt.

AVOID FINANCIAL LIFE REGRETS

#1
97% WOULD HAVE BEEN HAPPIER WITHOUT SO MUCH DEBT

#2
77% REGRET NOT LEARNING HOW TO INVEST

#3
85% WISH THEY HAD NOT CREATED THEIR SCHOOL DEBT

80% OF OLDER AMERICANS HAVE AT LEAST ONE FINANCIAL REGRET

Ninety-seven percent of people who live with debt believe they would be much happier in life if they never created it to begin with.*

Debts can easily take over every aspect of your life. Every waking minute can end up being spent either making money to pay your debts or worrying about paying your debts. Studies have also noted a strong link between unhappiness, health problems, depression, and accompanying debt—although they could not say which came first, the depression or the debt.[8] Debt also makes it much harder for you to build prosperity. If you could avoid the mistake of too much debt, it would make your life much more satisfying.

The next most common life regret involves investing.

A full 77% of Americans strongly regret not learning how to invest or not investing sooner in their lives.[9]

Investing is a vital financial independence concept you must learn before it is too late to be effective for you—as the benefits of investing occur over time. Learning when you are older reduces investing's effectiveness—although it is still worth doing. Investing early is a common path to creating wealth, and the earlier you can begin investing, the more prosperity you can create for yourself.

Now we can discuss the next most common financial life regret of younger people, which is accumulating student loan debt.

A full 85% of millennials who created student debt now regret doing so.[10]

Student loan debt is the Godzilla of all financial regrets for younger generations. If you search, "The most complained about debt of our younger generation," school debt will be the answer.

That is no surprise as school related loans just topped a trillion dollars nationwide. 85% of young people who created student debt regret doing so. Let me be quick to add, the younger generation said they do not regret obtaining an education, they just regret the debt they racked up to procure it.[11]

The sad part is, when these students created their school debt, they likely did not know or understand it would take them decades to pay it off. The average college debt ($20K to $39K) takes almost twenty years to pay off. The average student loan payment has been calculated to cost around $393 a month.[12] Of course, it will take much longer if you borrow more to obtain an advanced degree—possibly up to thirty years to pay off $60K or more.[13]

Essentially, you end up accruing interest on the interest until you begin making your student loan payments. This creates a growing payoff amount and a longer-lasting payment period. For example, if you owe just $1,000 on a student loan debt with a low 2.5% interest rate, and you make only the minimum payment allowed, it will take you five years to pay that debt off because the balance grows over time.[14]

Paying out that kind of money each month on student loans will have a significant, negative impact on your life, both now and in the future. Unfortunately, this debt could very easily impact your financial life forever. Consider this:

If you saved and invested the money you used to pay off your student loans, rather than repaying student loans over time, in twenty-five years you could easily have up to $500,000 or more—depending upon your return on investment (ROI).

One of the issues that make this difficult problem even worse is that students are finding starting salaries for graduates disappointing, and they are making much less money than they anticipated with their expensive degrees.[15] Many people feel that the advantage of a college degree is now much lower than it used to be because of the constant rising cost of education.[16] Also, a college degree's ROI is dependent upon the type of degree you obtain, where you get it, how much you paid for it, and the type of job and industry in which you begin working.

In 2022, the average cost to go away to college is around $53,949 per year. This includes just over $37,000 in tuition and about $17,000 in housing, according to studentloanplanner.com.[17] The cost of going away to college for a four-year degree, based on this data, will cost you or your parents over $2,000 a month for 10 years. You could easily assure future prosperity by investing that kind of money over time.

An even bigger problem arises for the students who began college and obtained a student loan, but then failed to graduate. Almost half of those who attend college (40%) do not finish their degrees.[18] Once they leave school, officially or unofficially, their student loan payments begin whether they graduated or not. Now they have all the handicaps of a student loan without any of the advantages of a degree. This information is vital to your future because at age thirty, the average millennial uses 45% of their total income just to pay their student loans. Therefore, they live in near poverty, with no savings and no opportunity to build prosperity in their immediate future.[19] This is not a good life plan!

Contrary to society's current message, you can obtain an education without any college debt! A Game-Winning Strategy!

AVERAGE SCHOOL DEBT
$20-39K

LOAN= 20 YEARS
AT $393 A MONTH

OR

INVEST THE SAME
AMOUNT & MAKE
$500K OR MORE!

That's a super important fact, even though it's not well pub-licized. The most common ways to obtain an education without debt include:

1. Obtain grants and scholarships.

2. Work for an employer that will pay part of your tuition and attend part-time or full-time such as:
   - Apple
   - Chick-Fil-A
   - Chipotle
   - McDonalds
   - Starbucks
   - Amazon

3. Join the U.S. military and utilize the GI Bill once your tour (typically four years) is complete.
4. Attend college part-time and pay as you go.
5. Attend a community college first to save money and pay as you go.
6. Go to a state school in your home state within driving distance of your family home to avoid housing costs.

I obtained a master's degree without taking on any school debt, by attending college part-time and taking advantage of my employer's tuition reimbursement program. My wife has completed her bachelor's degree and she has zero college debt because she took advantage of a scholarship for academics and tuition reimbursement from her employer. Our youngest child just graduated from business college with zero school debt by serving in the Navy for 4 years and then using his GI Bill. We are not the only ones. A full 42% of students who get a bachelor's degree graduate without any student debt.[20]

GRANTS & SCHOLARSHIPS

JOB WITH TUITION
REIMBURSEMENT

U.S. MILITARY SERVICE
& G.I. BILL

GOING PART TIME &
PAYING AS YOU GO

COMMUNITY COLLEGE

STATE SCHOOL
CLOSE TO HOME

Seth Berkowitz has no student debt! When he was in his junior year at the University of Pennsylvania, he realized there were few late-night sweet snacks available for students who were chronically up in the wee hours of the morning cramming for class the next day. To that end, Seth founded Insomnia Cookies, a company that delivers just-baked cookies (from his off-campus apartment) straight to customers' apartments or dorm rooms. A year later, the company had its first retail outlet in Syracuse, NY. A year after that, the company had a food truck with regular customers. In four years, they had twelve locations in various college towns. Now the company is franchised with over 100 locations and is still growing. Currently, the company is estimated to be worth around $500 million.[21] According to Seth, there is no time like the present to start your business, as starting a new business gets harder as you age because you have more responsibilities.[22]

There are numerous additional common financial regrets, but they are variations on the themes we just covered. For example, many people regret purchasing an expensive home because they are having trouble making their house payments.

I want more for you, and hopefully, you want more for yourself. You can avoid some of the experiences that put your life on a negative trajectory that is difficult to reverse by learning about others' experiences.

Cheat Codes:

When older Americans are interviewed, a common theme is they have regrets in life. They almost always include at least one financial regret that negatively impacted their lives. Typical regrets included:

- Creating too much debt
- Not saving money
- Not learning to invest
- Creating long-term school debt

You are young and can overcome your financial mistakes. It would be much easier on you, however, if you put some effort into learning about personal finance and avoid expensive financial lessons. This technique will set you up for future success.

Many people can work full-time and attend college part-time (such as my wife and me). Others work full time until they have some money saved, then they quit (or work part time) and go to college full-time until they run out of money and then repeat this process. Still others join the military and use their GI Bill to pay for college. Finally, you can work for employers that will either help pay your college debt or provide tuition reimbursement for those attending college now.

Up Next:

Now that we have talked about what to avoid, it is time to talk about what you should do! Keep reading to learn about the next steps necessary to create prosperity.

Online Money Game:

Try this game that demonstrates how to manage money and make financial decisions. https://payoff.practicalmoneyskills.com/

4

Conquering the Money Game's Five Levels

"Success will never be a big step in the future; success is small steps taken now." — **Jonathan Mårtensson, Swedish football superstar, net worth of $1 million**

S am Dogen went to work at an investment firm right out of college. He saved every dime he possibly could and budgeted his money closely. His philosophy was, "If it is not painful, you are not saving enough." He lived extremely modestly by living with several roommates. Also, in order to save money, he bought the cheapest used car he could find. By saving and investing half of every dime he made in a very aggressive mix of investments, he was able to become a millionaire at age twenty-eight. He also invested in his education without creating school debt. At twenty-eight years old, he quit his investment banking job and now runs his website, Financial Samurai at financialsamurai.com.

Without a comprehensive understanding of how everything works together, Sam Dogen's story might easily seem unachievable. You might wonder how a person could ever get to that level of wealth with an average job. When most people try to understand personal finance, they feel overwhelmed trying to absorb disconnected, seemingly unrelated pieces of information to create a system that will work for them. It is a huge subject, and most people don't even know where to begin studying to master it.

Luckily, I can show you exactly where to begin. There are five levels of the Money Game. The game is a stair-step system, much like a video game's multi-level structure. You must master the skills of the lower level to progress to the next. If you learn, understand, and utilize the financial information in these levels, you will improve your game play and increase your chances of excelling in the Money Game. If you don't master these levels, your chances of becoming financially independent decrease and you may never gain control of your financial life.

Master These Five Skill Levels to Win Your Money Game:

1. *Set financial and life goals*
2. *Create income from your job or businesses.*
3. *Budget your income*
4. *Save your money*
5. *Invest your savings regularly over time*

Goal Setting: The entire game should always begin with setting goals. Just seeing how life goes has never been a good strategy for either financial or over-all life success. Also, daydreaming about success, while never taking any concrete action, is an equally poor strategy. Quite frankly, this is what nearly everyone does, and it leads to less-than-ideal life outcomes. Instead, focus on your financial and personal goals.

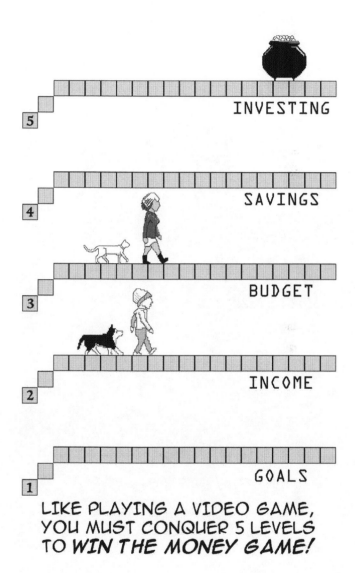

INVESTING

SAVINGS

BUDGET

INCOME

GOALS

LIKE PLAYING A VIDEO GAME,
YOU MUST CONQUER 5 LEVELS
TO *WIN THE MONEY GAME!*

Ideally, your financial goals are designed to support your life goals.

YOUR *FINANCIAL GOALS*
SHOULD SUPPORT YOUR
LIFE GOALS!

Creating Income: At the second level, you need to create an income stream, such as a job (see glossary in the back of book). The types of income streams you create to fund your life depend upon your goals, interests, and life objectives.

Budgeting: To obtain the best use or value from your income, you *must* budget. Unfortunately, only 33% of Americans bother to budget their income.[1]

> Not budgeting is by far the most common financial mistake in the world.[2]

Saving: One of the most critical budget categories is your savings, which is the next level of the Money Game. You will need savings to mitigate unexpected expenses and respond to life emergencies. Savings buffers life's many ups and downs, such as a job loss. Failure to save leads to excessive debt, financial hardship, and personal chaos in both your near and long-term future.

Jake Lyon began a career as a professional gamer. He played in the Overwatch League for the Houston Outlaws. Unlike a lot of other players who had no idea what they were doing with money, Jake saved 65% of his very large salary (exact amount undisclosed) from the beginning of his gaming career. Jake had saved so much that he retired in 2019 at twenty-three years old. He couldn't stay away from Overwatch, however, so he came back as a colorcastor or shoutcastor for eSports to narrate Overwatch games. From there, he tried coaching the Outlaws Overwatch team. He has since transitioned to a coach/player for the team. The point is, he saves and invests his income and does not randomly spend it. That makes sense for Jake because he started his college career as an economics major and he previously interned at the office of a financial advisor.[3] Jake also promotes financial literacy skills to his fellow players and encourages them to also save and invest their own earnings.

Investing: Once you have enough in savings to overcome most common life problems—like no job for six months or more—you need to begin investing your savings to create prosperity. Investing is a mighty force that uses the power of compounding interest to create prosperity (see Glossary). The point of all the lower levels is to get to this one, extremely powerful step.

It is the investing level of the game that will produce your future prosperity. The more money you have invested and the earlier you invested it, the more money you can potentially make.

Although being young will hinder you in the experience department, it is really a huge advantage to you in the investing department. Conversely, the longer you wait to start working on building prosperity, the harder this task becomes. If you use these steps right away, they can supercharge your finances for life.

Cheat Codes:

There are five levels of the Money Game. The game is a stair-step system, much like a video game's multi-level structure. You must master the skills of the lower level to progress to the next. Skipping a level will lead to poor outcomes. The 5 levels are:

1. Set goals
2. Create income
3. Budget
4. Save
5. Invest

This system organizes all personal finance into easy steps that anyone can understand. Everything in this system is also a mainstream financial concept or a best financial practice used by the wealthy (Warren Buffett, for example).

Up Next:

Now that you understand how these five levels work together to create prosperity, we can start increasing your knowledge about each individual step. Keep reading to learn how to supercharge your success and achieve more than you ever thought possible by using the power of goal setting.

Online Money Game:

In this game, you must figure out how to feed cats that grow by various compounding interest rates. This great game will teach you the finer points of compound interest and its power to change your future. https://www.ngpf.org/blog/math/math-monday-compound-interest/

5

The Best Game-Play Strategy is Goal Setting

"Life is what we make it, always has been, always will be."
— **Grandma Moses**

Born in 1860 as Anna Mary Moses, she officially began her painting career at the age of 78 and became a successful 20th-century American folk artist. Grandma Moses was born into a poor family and took a job at twelve years old as a live-in housekeeper for a rich family. Later, she and her husband worked on a dairy farm in Virginia. Long before she became famous, Moses had built a modest but secure financial life by managing her and her husband's dairy business income correctly. She always had a goal to create savings and make a certain level of income. Goal setting and very hard work were the cornerstones of her life.[1] These efforts left her reasonably happy and satisfied with her life long before she became a famous artist. Later in life, her popularity as a folk painter helped her to become a very wealthy woman (for her time) with a net worth of over $1.4 million.

If there is a magical ingredient to becoming financially independent, it is goal setting! Goal setting is an amazing system that puts you in control of your life and allows you to decide what you want, visualize your ideal outcomes, and push your visions into the real world. You create tangible results from what initially began only as an idea in your mind. This powerful process will not only enhance your professional life, but it can also improve your personal and financial situations as well.

> We are the only creatures on the planet with the power of visualizing an outcome we desire and then bringing that vision into the real world.

In the personal finance world, goal setting is vital. Those who become financially independent almost always do so because of planning and effort. It is a rare occurrence for someone to become wealthy accidentally. In fact, 92% of those who are wealthy made an explicit goal to become so. They also took the steps needed to create the result they envisioned and were successful in bringing their goals to fruition.[2] This statistic gives you a snapshot into how important goal setting and intentional actions will be in your future.

Here are the steps involved in goal setting for prosperity:
1. Determine what you want in life.
2. Write down your goals.
3. Connect emotionally with your goals.
4. Evaluate where you stand today in relation to your goals.
5. Research how to achieve your goals.
6. Create a written action plan to achieve your goals.
7. Set a timeline for obtaining each goal.

8. Monitor your progress.

9. Adjust your plan as needed to overcome the inevitable problems that will block your path.

10. Celebrate your accomplishments.

HUMANS ARE THE ONLY CREATURES WITH THE NEARLY *MAGICAL POWER* OF VISUALIZING AN OUTCOME & THEN BRINGING THAT OUTCOME INTO OUR PHYSICAL WORLD!

THIS POWER ALLOWS YOU TO CONTROL THE DIRECTION & OUTCOMES IN YOUR LIFE.

Daymond John, one of the co-stars on the hit show Shark Tank, has a very interesting back-story. Daymond grew up in Queens, New York. While many of his peers were ending up dead or in jail by the age of twenty-one, Daymond had other ideas for his life. He set success and wealth goals for his life at an early age. After deciding upon his goals and visualizing them, he wrote them down. Daymond then reviewed his goals every morning and then again at bedtime. He once wrote himself a check, to be cashed later, for $102,345,086.32 which he was able to cover by age thirty.[3]

Daymond was the founder of a HipHop clothing company called FUBU. He began his business by selling hats on a NY street corner. Later, the FUBU brand was created by Daymond and his mother who produced their first clothing inventory on sewing machines in their home. His understanding of the HipHop culture enabled him to provide customers the style they wanted. FUBU grew into a clothing powerhouse and now has a $6 billion valuation.

Two important lessons can be gained from Daymond's story. The first lesson is that setting ambitious goals can really pay off. In Chapter One, I told my story of setting a goal of obtaining a million dollars and that is what I later achieved. Daymond, however, set his goals on becoming a multimillionaire. Through goal setting and continual effort, he crushed his long-held goal.[4] The second lesson is the more effort and commitment you are willing to put into achieving your goal, the better your chances of success. Consider Daymond. How does your effort stack up against his? Effort is, and will always be, an essential ingredient to achieve your goals. I know lots of people who have big goals but give them no effort at all. I don't think their desires even qualify as goals.

One of the keys to goal setting, not often discussed, is picking goals that excite you so that you can emotionally connect with them and maintain your enthusiasm over the long haul. Your enthusiasm will help you remain motivated and persevere in the face of inevitable roadblocks along your path.

> Encountering difficulties on your journey is the norm for every goal achiever and does not mean you simply get to quit. Instead, it means you adjust your plan and refine your strategies to overcome the latest obstacle blocking your path.

One of the beginning steps in goal setting is figuring out where you stand right now. For a financial goal, a good way to start is to determine your current financial standing, which is summarized by your net worth (see Glossary).

To determine your net worth, you will need to know your total assets and liabilities. Your asset total is the value of all your asset values added together. Then, list all your liabilities for the total amount you owe. Then subtract your liabilities from your assets. This gives you your net worth. As a very easy example, let's say you are staying with your parents, but you have a job and make your own money. Now, let's say you have a car worth $1,000. The only loan you must pay each month is your car loan. That car loan has a balance of $500 that still needs to be paid. Your net worth would be:

$1,000 assets - $500 liabilities = $500 total assets.

You have a net worth of $500 in this simplified example.

When you graduate high school, your net worth is likely to be zero or very close to zero. You might even have a negative net worth value. No worries. You can change this in short order with intentional, directed effort.

You need an informed written plan (goal setting point #6) to guide your efforts to obtain the results you need. The best format for a plan is to write your goal at the top of a piece of paper. Under your written goal, write your plan to achieve that goal. Also list multiple subgoals, benchmarks or accomplishments you must obtain on the path to your goals. This is a good way to organize your written plan in a linear fashion and will help you stay on track.

To gather the information needed to write an informed plan, you will need to do some research. If you have an incorrect understanding of how your goals will be obtained, you will waste a lot of time, money, and energy. Overcoming this problem (lack of Money Game experience), will require some reading and studying on your part to learn financial management's best practices. (See books "Recommended for Further Study" in the back of the book.) You'll incorporate the important concepts you learn from your research into your written plan described above. That written plan will guide your future efforts and increase your chances of success.

All goals must include a realistic time frame for achievement (write the date next to your goal at the top of the paper). Without time frames for action and achievement, it's not a goal. It's only a wish or daydream.

Once you have your written goals with appropriate time frames, take deliberate action to advance your written plan and achieve your goals on your schedule. If you achieve your goals a little later than planned, that's okay. The accomplishments and benefits are still real and tangible.

Writing down your goals has real power in the Money Game and is the first step in creating the future you want, rather than stumbling into an unfortunate situation due to your failure to plan. Writing down a goal gives your thoughts a physical presence in this world. Its biggest benefit is focusing your mind on the process. After I write down my goals, I usually tape them to my bathroom mirror, which I strongly recommend. There is no escaping them when you do that! You look at your goals as you get ready to take on each day, which helps you focus on the desired objectives and outcomes.

YOU MUST TAKE
ACTION TO MAKE
YOUR GOALS A
REALITY!

Here is a list to create potential financial goals and subgoals. (For more ideas order the Escape Debt Prison Workbook on Amazon.)

Goal:_____

Time:_____

Sub Goal: _____

Time:_____

Sub Goal:_____

Time:_____

Sub Goal:_____

Time:_____

Plan:

_____

_____

_____

_____

_____

_____

_____

Larry Faulkner

One of your success strategies with goal achievement should be to maintain a positive attitude in the face of inevitable setbacks that will occur during the pursuit of your goals.[5] Positive thinking isn't magic. You will suffer setbacks and even outright failures. This is a fact, and it is very normal. Without a positive attitude, you will be unable to overcome obstacles and push through life's disappointments to progress toward your goals. Pessimism never helped anyone accomplish any significant goal! Your attitude is always an important component of prosperity creation or any other goal you undertake.

For example, the National Federation of State High School Associations says that if a high school football coach is given a choice between a player with more talent or a great attitude, they would absolutely take the student with the best attitude. It is their belief that attitude will enhance the team's chemistry which is the magic ingredient for success.[6]

Here is a trick I use to keep myself positive: I go out of my way to encourage and help others achieve their goals, which keeps me in a positive frame of mind and allows me to make many friends and connections. You could do the same on your journey to create the future you desire. After all, everyone could use cheerleaders in their lives!

Cheat Codes:

Goal setting is an amazing process that allows you to control the direction and conditions of your life. Those who use this system are happier and more financially sound than those who do not. For goal setting to work effectively, however, it is essential that you understand what you want, otherwise you will waste a lot of time and effort. You increase your chances of accomplishing your goals if you utilize a more formal process such as writing your goals down with an accompany plan on how you will achieve them. Those who use and commit to this process have created amazing results that have transformed their lives for the better.

Up Next:

Income is very important. Keep reading to learn how to maximize the amount of income you can obtain.

Online Game:

Try this financial simulator to help you create money goals and a plan to achieve them: https://projectionlab.com

6

Creating Game-Winning Income

"Your economic security does not lie in your job; it lies in your own power to produce—to think, to learn, to create, to adapt. That's true financial independence. It's not having wealth; it's having the power to produce wealth." — **Stephen Covey, best-selling author, businessman, multi-millionaire, educator and highly respected motivational speaker**

There was a point in my life when I became very disillusioned with my policing career. Everything about my job seemed irritating to me. Since this was my chosen mission in life, this caused me quite a bit of confusion and concern. After some deep self-reflection, I realized the problem was not the police department or the job I was doing at all. Instead, the problem was me. The real problem was my inner feeling that I had "limited" myself. I had trapped myself into a narrow job by my own lack of marketable qualifications and experiences outside this narrow field. I came to the realization that if something in the department were to go wrong and I somehow lost my current job, I had few workplace skills and abilities to market to another employer. That situation had to change, and I set about creating goals and a plan to do just that.

I set various goals to increase my skill set which soon led to obtaining a graduate degree in science/data-based policing. I also obtained a variety of certifications and management trainings. Once I increased my skills, these feelings of being trapped evaporated.

Later, when opportunities presented themselves, I used my skill enhancements to spring forward in my department. Soon I was a division manager of a mixed segment of detectives, police officers, and civilian employees, with a multi-million-dollar budget. Just as important to me, my salary was now much higher, which allowed my wife and I to save nearly half our combined income.

The moral of the story is that I realized I had an over-reliance on my current job. Such an overreliance reduces financial security and makes you more vulnerable to economic downturns or something unexpectedly going awry with your employer. Just as Stephen Covey said, your real ability to generate income lies entirely in your own skills and abilities. If yours are deficient, you must increase your abilities to be a top-level player in the Money Game.

The Money Game contains almost limitless ways to create income. The methods we choose are heavily influenced by our personal history, our culture and the values we hold. The two primary methods of earning income are working at a job for a wage or creating your own business.

Getting A Job:

Let's discuss the culturally preferred path for Americans, which is to find a job. You do this by getting an employer (company) to hire you. The idea is to get better and better jobs as you gain experience, thereby significantly increasing your income over time.

In our culture, a college education is the culturally accepted path to better paying jobs. Back in your parents' time, this was absolutely true! Our society, however, is shifting and this cultural norm is no longer an absolute. Skills are becoming highly valuable to employers. Of course, having both skills and education remain the undisputed gold standard in employability.

When it comes to a job, how much you make significantly impacts your current lifestyle and your ability to create future prosperity. It is in your best interest to obtain the highest wage the market will bear for your labor. Your constant challenge is to maximize how much money you make from your employer. Conversely, it is in your employer's best interest to pay you as little as possible while obtaining the maximum benefit from your labor.

Your best techniques to obtain higher pay include:

- Make the effort to ask for a raise.
- Jump to a competitor for more pay.
- Make sure you display a positive attitude in the workplace.
- Get promoted to a higher-paying position.
- Develop yourself in areas such as education and special-ized training, to increase your value as an employee.

You should not hesitate to ask for more money—at the correct time, of course. To be successful at obtaining more money, you need to show up with significant reasons and real numbers demon-strating why you deserve a raise. Also, don't just show up in your boss's office one day out of the blue. Get on your supervisor's calendar for a meeting. That way, he or she won't be irritated or distracted by everyday work problems. This will also give you a chance to organize your material for an orderly presentation. Give a short verbal (or written) presentation with numbers and facts. If you schedule the meeting correctly and come prepared, you will be heads above your coworkers' efforts to get a raise.

THOSE WHO GET THE BEST PAY AT WORK:

- CONTINUAL SELF-IMPROVEMENT
- DO MORE WORK THAN OTHERS
- POSITIVE LEADERS
- MOST KNOWLEDGEABLE ABOUT THEIR JOB
- LOOK FOR OPPORTUNITIES TO GET PROMOTED

Keep your eyes open for opportunities at other companies to possibly snag a similar job with higher pay. Just keep in mind, the hassles and expense of changing employers (for a small raise) is not usually worth the effort unless the new job offers substantially more advancement opportunities.

You also increase your value in the workplace by being a positive leader. Apathetic people are everywhere in the workforce. In any workplace, there are also usually one or two downright negative employees and they do not use their influence for good. They seed discord, rebellion and create needless problems. As an employer, I was always looking to unload my negative employees at the first opportunity. If you actively seek ways to further your company's objectives, however, you zoom to the top of your boss's favorite list.

Getting promoted in the organizational chain is also a solid strategy to make more money. The higher you can climb, the higher your salary. Another benefit of getting promoted is you usually gain more freedom regarding how you do your job. To go up the organizational structure usually requires a mix of talents that include the ability to navigate office politics, the right educational and training qualifications, and excellent performance reviews.

As an employee seeking to maximize his or her value, continual self-improvement is also required to grow within your organization. Even so, qualified people are passed over every day for promotions. Be patience and persistence; However, organizational upward mobility is not an objective that works for everyone.

Self-development is always a good technique to increase your value in the job market. You can always choose to become good at technical tasks that few others can do, which really ramps up your value to any company. If it's a task or job that others find difficult, it increases your value to an employer even more. Additionally, most employers are impressed if you continue your education. At the very least, it will make you more employable at another workplace.

Creating A Business:

In other cultures, it is normal for people to strike out on their own and start their own businesses. This is true in South Korea, where one in four people start their own businesses.[1] In America, the skills you need to create an entrepreneurial life are typically not provided in high school, which is a shame as a recent survey indicated that nearly 60% of high school students want to start their own businesses.[2]

Sure, you can get a business education in college, but most of that education (not all, I admit) is geared toward making you employable. Some high schools are lucky enough to have national organizations like FBLA (Future Business Leaders of America) and DECA (Distributive Education Clubs of America), which teach business principles. Opinions on their effectiveness for teaching actual business skills, however, vary.

A few quality summer programs are available for high school students, including the Management and Technology Summer Institute (M&TSI) at the University of Pennsylvania for high school juniors and seniors. This three-week program helps young adults develop business ideas that they can then pitch on the hit ABC show Shark Tank. Another summer program is Launch X, an online 6-week program for high school juniors and seniors that provides teams of students with various support services to help build a product.

If you are a young adult or just want to skip high school business classes and learn with adults, excellent low-cost business training classes (even personal mentors) are offered by your local SCORE office (Service Corp of Retired Executives). SCORE is a nonprofit organization, dedicated to educating future business owners. I've had very positive experiences with this organization and have utilized their services and business training.

If you would like to access your local SCORE Office, go to this website and enter your zip code to obtain the contact information. Sign up for classes or see what business resources are available to assist you: https://www.score.org

Studies show that most young, successful entrepreneurs typically learned business values and skills at home and leverage those skills into start-up businesses.[3] If that is not the case for you, that doesn't have to be a barrier. You can always obtain free business education from a variety of sources. Plenty of education is available in various business books or in seminars at your local library. These days, you can also learn virtually any business skill you might need online. You are only limited by your initiative and desire to learn.

Self-Esteem Also Influences Income:

One final point about earning more income while working at a job. Those who have high self-esteem earn more money, get better jobs, are more successful and create more wealth than those who lack self-esteem. *Science Daily* cites multiple studies that show a direct correlation between teenagers with higher self-esteem and adults who have more wealth later in life.[4]

Earlier, I mentioned that I finally came to the realization that if I wanted a better, more successful life, it was entirely up to me. No one else was going to do it for me, so I was going to have to put forth the effort to create the life I envisioned. Up to that point, I hadn't put much effort into many important aspects of my life. Of course, more effort almost always creates better results. When I increased my effort, it created better outcomes. Better outcomes, in turn, improved my results and better results created higher self-esteem.

MORE EFFORT ALMOST ALWAYS CREATES BETTER RESULTS

GREATER EFFORT CAN EVEN DEFEAT THOSE WHO HAVE MORE TALENT!

The takeaway is work on your self-esteem because it is very important to your personal life and financial future. One of the easiest ways to increase your self-esteem is by successfully completing a series of small tasks. New research shows that concentrating on small, achievable goals in the beginning is a great confidence builder, self-esteem booster, motivator, and general facilitator of future success. [5]

If you have self-esteem issues, which is actually pretty common, you can work on overcoming them. More effort and the success that typically follows can help self-esteem issues. In my book *From Money Disaster to Prosperity: The Breakthrough Formula*,[6] I discuss how past experiences can sabotage you, and I go into more detail on how to change your perspectives to become more successful.

If your problem is beyond self-esteem and extends into serious depression, then please talk to your doctor, and don't hesitate to call this number for immediate assistance should you consider harming yourself:

Suicide & Crisis Hotline
Call 988

Income Nearly Always Creates Income Tax:
Now let's cover an important, yet more mundane subject matter—taxes. You are obligated to pay taxes (federal, state in some cases, and local) on all your income annually. Your income tax form and a subsequent payment is due by April 15th of the following year. You can find the federal forms you need (likely the 1040-EZ) and instructions on how to pay your taxes at https://www.irs.gov/

forms-pubs/about-form-1040-ez.[7] There is also online assistance available by phone if you have questions or need help. Local tax preparers may also conduct classes at the local library or business center that you can attend for free or little cost.

If you work for an employer, they withhold your taxes in your weekly or bi-weekly check. If you have your own business, you must withhold and submit the taxes yourself. Those who are self-employed and are making a good deal of money typically pay taxes quarterly. It is a good idea, therefore, to determine your approximate tax liability and save some of it to make your quarterly tax payments to avoid possible penalties for underpayment.

Your annual income tax is usually paid on a graduating scale, meaning the less you make annually, the less tax you owe. In fact, low earners traditionally even get money back via an income tax credit.

Paying your income tax annually is a legal requirement.

Not paying taxes can be considered a crime, depending on the circumstances. At the very least, there may be steep fines, penalties and interest for not paying or for failing to file your taxes on time. Not filing can have long-lasting, negative consequences. Hiding income or fraudulently listing a lower income is a crime that may land you in court and maybe in jail. Paying your taxes on an annual basis is a requirement no matter what else happens in life.

In my experience, I have found the IRS reasonably easy to work with, and they are perfectly willing to create a payment plan if you find that you cannot pay your annual bill. If they find a mistake in your tax return, they are usually pretty good about working out a solution with you. To clarify, "working" with the IRS means they will probably charge you a fine and penalty in addition to the amount you owe or failed to pay.

Cheat Codes:

This chapter covered the fact that our cultural upbringing has a surprising impact on how we view money and the ways we earn it. Most formal education is geared toward training you to work for others. You learned that to increase your income you need to increase your skills, your training, your effort, and your self-esteem. If you wish to work for yourself as an entrepreneur, it will be up to you to educate yourself. Finally, paying taxes is an absolutely legal requirement. Failing to file and pay taxes could even be considered a crime for which you can be jailed. Luckily, filing taxes isn't that hard, and online instructions and assistance are available.

Up Next:

If one income stream is good in the Money Game, then two are even better. Find out how game strength is ramped up by income stream creation.

Online Game:

Check out this online game that advertises itself as the "world's best" career aptitude test: https://www.careerexplorer.com/career-test/

7

Ramp Up Game Play with Multiple Income Streams

"Many small streams form a big river." – **Swedish Proverb**

Narrow-minded people insist that any new information they receive confirms what they already know or what they already believe (a.k.a. confirmation bias). Not much growth can occur within this mindset. However, people who are open to learning new things can incorporate new knowledge into a new way of thinking. Take Warren Buffet for example:

Billionaire investor, bestselling author, philanthropist, and entrepreneur Warren Buffet was born into a middle-class family in Omaha, Nebraska during the Great Depression. Buffet is known for being one of the best investors in the world and currently has a net worth of over $109 billion. He is also the founder and CEO of Berkshire Hathaway, a holding corporation that owns controlling shares in many other companies. Warren was interested in money at an early age. He bought his *first stock at the age of 11 and made his first real estate investment at the age of 14. Today, one of his most basic principles of wealth is to never rely on only one income. One income can easily be interrupted, leaving you in dire financial straits, which is why he encourages everyone to create multiple income streams.*

My intention is to expand your mind and tell you what you may not already know. For example, did you know that creating multiple income streams is actually a common practice among the rich to win their Money Game? A study in 2017 determined three income streams seem to be the breakthrough point for creating real prosperity—with the very wealthy having more than three income streams.

- 65% of self-made millionaires had at least three income streams.[1]
- 29% of the very rich had five or more income streams.[2]

Financial independence is most easily achieved by creating a regular flow of money into your budget from several sources. The more income streams you build, the more freedom you create in your life. Also, the more independent your income streams are from one another, the more secure your financial life becomes.

Here are a few examples of income streams:

- Income from a job
- Income from a second job
- Income from investments
- Income from reselling merchandise
- Income from a business you created
- Income from hobbies
- Income from one of the military branches
- Income from additional sources

3 INCOME STREAMS:

THE BREAKTHROUGH POINT FOR CREATING FINANCIAL INDEPENDENCE!

CREATING MULTIPLE INCOME STREAMS IS A COMMON PRACTICE OF THE RICH!

If you ever get married or cohabitate, your spouse should also create multiple income streams. The more income streams the two of you create, the more financially secure you become. This is a very important concept, especially now when jobs come and go every day. Today's great job can be a distant memory in a just a short time. Two income streams can provide a huge opportunity to boost your financial security, especially if both salaries are not required to pay debts.

Young millionaire and entrepreneur Charlie Chang learned the value of multiple income streams by necessity after he was turned down for medical school. He was forced to change career paths and had to pursue other avenues to create income. Charlie decided to create a business around financial education and coaching. Like many others in this book, he attracted customers to his classes and products via short videos on TikTok, YouTube and Instagram. His business took off and one of his videos went viral right after the pandemic. Eventually, Charlie created a variety of income streams that made him a millionaire, and his wealth is still growing at fast clip today.

Charlie Chang's Amazing Income Streams:

- Affiliate marketing: Charlie has product links in his videos. If viewers purchase products via his links, he is paid a commission.
- Brand sponsorship: When Charlie endorses products and recommends those products to others, he is paid.
- YouTube ads: Charlie puts an ad for a product on one of his videos and is paid per click for this advertising.
- Online financial courses
- Coaching others on how to make more money or how to better handle the money they already have.[3]

My wife and I have developed a half-dozen income streams, which allow us to no longer depend on jobs to pay the few monthly bills we have. Some of our income streams require effort on our part to maintain, but others require little maintenance.

Our streams:
- Larry's state pension
- Larry's investment income
- Income for publishing financial education products
- Lisa's part-time nursing job
- Lisa's investment income
- Contract jobs like coaching, teaching, and consulting

These income streams represent our efforts to date. We are working on plans to create even more, not because we must create more income streams, but because we love creating them.

Income streams that don't require much effort are considered "passive income streams." Of course, no one simply hands you a passive income stream. You must go out and build them.

Common examples of common passive income streams include:
- Writing e-books
- YouTuber
- Social media influencer
- Selling informational products
- Affiliate marketing (Selling a product through blogs or vlogs when an influencer promotes a product and provides an affiliate link to their audience.)
- Creating an app
- Rental properties

Unfortunately, none of the above income streams are actually passive in the strictest sense. The term "passive income stream" can be misleading. For instance, I have quite a bit of experience with the first item on the above list. Writing an e-book is a pretty active endeavor! You must research a topic, write the book, edit it, make corrections, and then have it edited a second time. Of course, you then need to create (or have someone create) a specialized e-book layout and the cover. Once the e-book is finally complete, the really hard work begins. Like every other product in the world, you must market and sell your e-book. Nothing about this process is passive, especially if your goal is to create income. The "passive income" part occurs through book sales, after you've put all the effort in to creating the book. Book royalties may be paid out as long as the book continues to sell.

Real estate and rental properties are also often considered passive income streams but require quite a bit of effort—maintenance issues, tenant management and marketing your properties—all go into the real estate rental business. The individuals I know who manage rental properties must work very hard—putting in time, labor, planning, marketing, and sales—to succeed even marginally. Later, when the real estate business grows, they are able to hire a full-time crew for maintenance, repairs, and new projects, making it somewhat passive.

Except for financial investments that produce a regular income, there are very few passive income streams. The only true passive income streams we have include a large investment portfolio and my State of Ohio pension for my years of service as a police officer. Of course, the pension took 32 years to build. So even though it is passive now, it took a while to build it.

An investment portfolio is simply a collection or a basket of different investment types of assets such as stocks, bonds, mutual funds, real estate, and other assets held in an investment account or group of accounts (see Glossary).

The potential flow of money from your investments can be quite large. Also, it takes very little effort to maintain an investment portfolio once it is set up. The very point of creating a diverse investment portfolio is to generate income for your future. That income stream can flow into your bank account when you are ready. Once it is set up, it will require minimal time and effort on your part to maintain—as opposed to working at your job or at a side business. That doesn't mean you should necessarily quit working. Instead, it means you have some control over your life and can decide what you will do or not do instead of an employer dictating it.

Here is a great example of an investment related passive income stream:

Assuming you have at least $1,000,000 in your investment portfolio, 4% (traditionally considered the amount you can remove without harming its growth) can provide you a average of $40,000 each year, in addition to any other income streams you have already built. As your portfolio grows, it can create even more income. Typically, a good mix of investments will bring 6% to 10% a year, which creates money for you and money to create more investment growth.

The math: $1,000,000 x 4% (or .04) = $40,000

When the wealthy finally get around to using their money, they never spend the million(s) they made over the years. Instead, the wealthy spend only the interest their money generates, which enables them to protect their golden goose ($1,000,000+) so it can keep laying golden eggs throughout their lives and beyond. If they were to spend more than the interest their million(s) generated, it would kill their income stream and the cash flow would drop and then eventually dry up. To put it another way:

THE MOST IMPORTANT PASSIVE INCOME STREAM IS AN INVESTMENT PORTFOLIO.

$1,000,000

4%

= $40,000 ANNUALLY

YOU CAN REMOVE 4% ANNUALLY WHILE STILL ALLOWING YOUR PORTFOLIO TO CONTINUE GROWING!

The golden goose is much more valuable than any of the golden eggs it lays.

INVESTMENT PORTFOLIO = GOOSE WHO LAYS GOLDEN EGGS!

THE GOOSE IS MORE VALUABLE THAN ANY OF ITS GOLDEN EGGS! PROTECT YOUR GOLDEN GOOSE!

Using the same method, your income stream from your investments becomes sustainable and renewable. As you age, 4% of a larger investment portfolio generates larger annual payments. You can soon remove around $50,000 annually, then $60,000 and so on, without damaging your awesome income-generating machine.

Cheat Codes:

Confirmation bias is when you believe something to be true and accept the evidence that supports your view but reject the evidence that indicates your view is wrong. This is a common problem in the area of personal finance and prevents growth.

Creating multiple income streams is a common practice of the wealthy. Millionaires typically have three income streams or more. Although many income streams are promoted as being passive, that is rarely the case. The most common passive income streams include investment income and pension income. If you have a partner, they should be involved in creating income streams as well.

Up Next:

To keep your income safe and use it to fund your life, you will need some important knowledge about financial institutions. Keep reading to learn about the banking system, how to keep your money safe, avoid pesky banking fees, and keep your wealth working for you.

Online Game:

Try creating an innovative startup company in this simulation game: http://thefounder.biz

8

The Game's Many Financial Institutions

"Business and life are like a bank account—you can't take
out more than you put in." — **William Feather**

William Feather was a successful businessman, entrepreneur, printer,
editor, publisher, and popular writer who was born in New York,
but moved to Cleveland, Ohio to be near family. He began his career
working for the Cleveland Press as a reporter. Later, he started his own
printing and publishing business. Feather produced catalogues, magazines, brochures, corporate annual reports and various books. He was a
talented writer who had unique views on life, such as you should look
at life like an adventure. He developed a very popular magazine, The
William Feather Magazine. He had an interest in business and much
of his writing related to business and personal finance topics. He is still
known today for his quirky money quotes in the magazines and books he
wrote. He had a net worth of nearly $5 million at the time of his death.

Once you have paychecks coming in on a regular basis, you
are going to need a place to stash your cash. Understanding the

financial infrastructure you must work within is an essential Money Game step. Skipping this lesson will handicap your game play. You need to know how to use financial institutions to serve your best interests rather than the bank's best interest.

Banks are a vital component of modern life. (In general, I use the term bank to also include credit unions and online banks.) They help make commerce possible. Financial institutions allow us to electronically transfer funds between banks through their automated clearing house (ACH) to pay our bills and buy the many items we need, which are actually bank-to-bank transfers at their core. Banking is typically safe and secure even when done electronically. Plus, if someone steals cash from you by removing your funds from your bank account, the bank will likely reimburse you for the loss.

You will need to create two types of accounts. The first account is a checking account, named after the old-school process of writing checks and keeping a paper and pen balance on a ledger. You will use your checking account to pay your monthly and weekly bills. Today, most bills are paid by automatically having an amount transferred from your checking account on a recurring monthly date to your approved vendors. Bills are also paid by electronic fund transfers (EFTs) or Person-To-Person (PTP) payment systems. Money is routed from your checking account to those you choose by using mobile payment applications like PayPal, Venmo, and Zelle (see Glossary).

The next account is a savings account where you stash your emergency fund. Unlike a checking account where money is constantly flowing in and out, you deposit money into a savings account to keep it secure for a longer period of time, yet still have easy access to the funds for emergencies. You will fund both your checking and your savings accounts by using direct deposit from your employers or transfer funds from your checking account to your savings account.

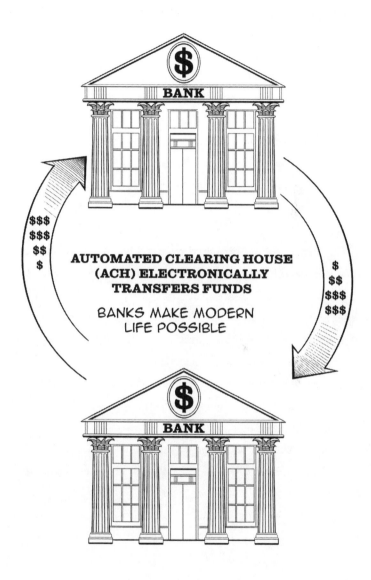

Three types of financial institutions that are the most common for our day-to-day use:

Commercial Bank

A commercial bank accepts your deposits, keeps your money safe, and allows you to withdraw money by writing checks or through electronically transfers. Banks also loan money to their customers and to other businesses in the community. In exchange for loaning their funds, banks charge customers an interest rate to make a profit (see Glossary).

Almost all banks became insured after the Great Depression in the early 1930s. During the Great Depression, bank runs (where depositors flocked to the bank to remove all their money at once) were very common due to news about bank failures in other towns. This created a panic that fed upon itself, fueled by the poor economic conditions in the country at that time. Since 1933, bank deposits have been insured by the Federal Deposit Insurance Corporation (FDIC), in an attempt to prevent future bank runs. Bank runs can destroy financial institutions because banks cannot possibly pay out all their depositors in one day.

For banking services, you should only deal with financially insured institutions. The FDIC will insure your money up to $250,000 against bank failures which actually happens more than you think. For example, several bank failures occurred in 2023, including Silicon Valley Bank and Signature Bank. The FDIC only insures checking or savings accounts, not the investments a bank might make on your behalf. Several bank failures occurred in 2023, including Silicon Valley Bank and Signature Bank.

1930's GREAT DEPRESSION
CREATED RUMORS ABOUT BANKS GOING BROKE!

BANK RUNS:

1. WHEN CUSTOMERS ALL RUN TO THE BANKS & DEMAND THEIR MONEY.

2. BANKS DON'T HAVE ENOUGH CASH TO PAY EVERYONE AT ONCE.

3. THE BANKS THEN DEFAULT & GO BROKE!

4. THE RUMORS SPREAD, FUELING MORE PEOPLE TO RUN TO THE BANKS.

5. CAUSING MORE BANKS TO COLLAPSE.

THIS CYCLE SPARKED A PANIC AND KILLED MANY BANKS!

TODAY:

BANKS ARE NOW INSURED SO YOUR MONEY *CAN'T* DISAPPEAR.

FDIC
INSURES CUSTOMERS UP TO $250K IN EACH ACCOUNT

BANK INSURANCE POLICY:

FEDERAL DEPOSIT INSURANCE CORPORATION

FDIC

For a vast majority of investments, there are no guaranteed results—just levels of risk that range from low to high. (See Chapter 15 for investments and risks.)

Credit Unions:

Credit unions are nonprofit financial institutions that mutually benefit members (called owners, depositors, or shareholders). You join by depositing money and, theoretically at least, you have a say in how the financial institution is run. Members are elected to the board of directors who choose the chief executive officer (credit union manager). Fees and interest rates charged for loans are usually less than those found at commercial banks. Credit unions need only make enough to fund their day-to-day operations. Our family uses credit unions whenever possible because, typically, you are treated better because you are a part owner of the financial institution. Credit unions used to be restricted to individuals working in a particular industry or people who live in a specific geographical area. These rules have been loosened, and most credit unions have dropped these qualifying requirements. You can now become a member of virtually any credit union in your neighborhood.

A separate group, The National Credit Union Administration (NCUA) administers (manages) the National Credit Union Share Insurance Fund (NCUSIF), which is an insurance on your savings and checking accounts. The NCUA insures these accounts at the same level as FDIC insures accounts at banks. Again, for cases of theft or fraud involving your account, this is handled by the credit union itself. NCUA only covers credit union failures.

Most credit unions are part of a nationwide shared branching system, which is a national network of credit unions.

Shared branching means you can walk into any participating shared branching credit union and route a deposit to your account at your credit union, make a withdrawal or pay funds to a third party, usually at no cost. Automated teller machines (ATMs) are also connected to shared branching sites and money can be deposited or withdrawn at a low to no cost.

Online Banks:

Online banks are quickly growing their customer base because they provide convenient, 24-hour access from your mobile device with usually the same FDIC protection as a commercial bank. You can electronically deposit checks and pay bills right from your phone or computer. The fees are typically less than traditional brick-and-mortar banks because online banks are not maintaining physical branches. They also typically offer lower interest rates on the loans they make to their customers. Always compare fees, however, to see if they are actually lower or the advertised rate is just a gimmick (more about this in the next chapter).

A drawback of online banking is that you can rarely get customer service assistance if something goes wrong and you need to talk with an actual person to fix your problem. Also, to obtain cash, you can use an ATM but will likely be charged an ATM fee. Online banks have no branches and are not part of a free interbank network for ATM transactions. Some online banks reimburse these ATM fees, but not all. Depositing cash into your online account could be a problem since not all ATMs will accept a cash deposit, although you can use the mobile deposit app typically for free.

Advantages & Disadvantages of Banking Institutions:

	Online Only	Credit Unions	Traditional Banks
Locations	Online only	Local branch & online; may be part of shared branch system and national ATM network	Local to national options; ATM network possible
Interest Rates Charged On Loans	Competitive to very low interest rates	Lowest fees	Highest
Interest Rate Paid to You on Savings Accounts	Best or highest interest rate paid on savings accounts	Next best	Worst
ATM Fees	ATM fee charged but may be reimbursed. Check with online bank policy.	None if ATM is part of their network; otherwise high fees. Always check ATM before using it to avoid fees.	None if ATM is part of their network; otherwise high fees. Always check ATM before using it to avoid fees.
Checking Account Maintenance Fees	Low or no fees	Maintenance fee with few exceptions. Ask for no-fee checking account.	Maintenance fee with few exceptions. Ask for no-fee checking account.
Insured	Varies widely, always check.	Almost all insured through NCUA	All insured through FDIC
Structure	For profit	Member run for member benefit	For profit

	Online Only	Credit Unions	Traditional Banks
Services	Varies widely	Most services are provided although commercial banking services (business services) may be limited	Wide menu of services and personalized assistance available.
Assistance If Something Goes Wrong	No personalized assistance available.	Best at providing assistance	Varies widely
Security	Very good as long as you use their security features and have a strong password that is not compromised	Excellent, plus they can provide personalized security and customize your security with notes on account	Fair to very good.
Technology	Very good but some services are limited	Varies widely as some credit unions lag on technology	Best
Versatility	Widely varies	Widely varies	Worst: They have strict rules and a corporate structure
Peercentage of Young Adult Customers	47%	22%	18%

Source: https://www.zdnet.com/finance/banking/bye-bye-megabank-more-young-adults-are-adopting-digital-banking-to-manage-their-money/[1]

Now let's talk about what will soon be the bane of your existence, especially if you are just starting out on your own with your finances. You may soon learn to despise the dreaded non-sufficient funds (NSF) fees or overdraft fees your financial institution is waiting to charge you should one of your financial transactions be rejected.

Here is the difference between these two fees:

- Overdraft Fee —If your financial institution fails to notice there are insufficient funds in your account and a transaction goes through, you will be charged a fee for spending more than is in your account.
- NSF Fee—If a bank catches that there are insufficient funds in your account and declines the transaction before it goes through, you are still charged a fee called an NSF fee.

If you have insufficient funds, no matter how brief that period might be, you will be charged a fee if a transaction (withdrawal) is attempted. The fees can range from $30 to $50 or even more in some cases. There are so many ways to overdraw (overdraft) your account and I have done nearly all of them in my younger days.

Here is a quick summary of my various misadventures:

- Write a check (or use an app to pay an amount over the money that is in your account, also called "bouncing a check")
- Make a withdrawal of more money than is in the account (overdraft)
- Failure to adjust/stop an automatic bill payment and then overdraw your account.

- Use your ATM card to withdraw more money than is in your account or purchase something with your ATM card, which costs more money than you have in your account.

There were no EFT payments when I was a young man, but if there were, I am sure I would have overdrawn my account using that method as well. All of these methods of overdraft are fairly straightforward. Each of them is clearly your fault because you made an obvious error.

Now let's consider some other overdraft situations that are a little less clear concerning who is at fault. Once again, I have also been involved in each and every one of these:

- ATM fees that put you into overdraft when you did not know there was an ATM charge
- Direct deposit paycheck being "delayed" due to an ACH problem or payday occurring during a holiday period
- Even though a check was deposited, and a receipt reflected a new, higher balance, the money has not been officially transferred into your account, and the deposit is delayed due to a problem with old-school checks or the ACH system
- Being charged a bank fee without your knowledge, which then created an overdraft on your account and can lead to additional overdrafts.

As a young person just starting out in the financial world, you are like a lamb going to the slaughter. If you are not careful, a bank may bleed you dry with their fees that boost their bottom line while decimating yours. This usually happens when you can least afford it and when your finances are at a low point. Also, as a bonus, you'll receive a message from the bank telling you that your account is overdrawn, you will be charged and that future violations could result in your account being closed. Finally, merchants will also charge you a fee if your payment, check or EFT, is rejected due to insufficient funds.

Thankfully, there are solutions that go beyond paying closer attention to your balance.

Six strategies to avoid the overdraft fee trap:

1. Financially plan for the future. By and large, people fail to financially plan ahead.[2] They are not looking weeks, months or longer into the future. Plan ahead to get ahead should be your motto! This practice helps you avoid financial disasters and surprises and helps you keep your goals firmly in focus.

2. You can age your money! Like fine wine, money is always best when it is aged. That means instead of using this month's wages to pay your bills, use last month's wages. In this example, you have aged your money a month. This assures that you are not living at the very edge of your financial resources. As soon as you can manage it, two to three months is an even better age for your money.

3. Link your checking account to your savings account. If your checking account becomes accidentally overdrawn, it pulls money from your savings to make up the shortage. This saves your NSF fees and merchant returned payment fees.

4. Create an emergency fund. An emergency fund is enough money to pay your bills for at least six months without income coming in. I personally think a year is better. This creates a big cushion for life's unexpected turns and disasters.

5. Find out if your bank will allow you a line of credit attached to your checking account that will automatically take money from the line of credit should a shortage occur. The only danger is if you start using the line of credit like a credit card. If you do, soon you will be right back where you started by overdrawing your line of credit account—which is even worse than overdrawing your checking account. Leave the line of credit for dire emergencies and pay off any balance immediately.

6. Pay the bank for overdraft protection. In some cases, this can be as much as $30 a month. Is it worth it? If you know in advance you will not be paying close attention to your balance, then likely it will save you money in the long run. You have to decide if the protection is worth $360 annually. Personally, I would rather have the $360 in my own account acting as an emergency fund.

Other Common Fees Banks Charge:

Checking Monthly Service Fee: Can be $10 to $15 a month. Sometimes you can avoid these fees by keeping a minimum balance or just asking for a fee free checking account.

ATM Fee: This is a fee you are charged if you use an ATM out of your banking ATM network. Learn which network they use and always check before you use the ATM. Try to stay within your network whenever possible.

Foreign Transaction Fees: Your ATM may (or may not) charge you a fee if you use an ATM in another country. Check with your banking institution. My wife and I use a credit card when we are out of the country that does not charge us foreign transaction fees. We pay the bill immediately upon our return home.

Account Closure Fee: If you open an account and then turn around and close it right away, usually within 90 days, your financial institution may charge you a fee. If this is something you plan to do, ask them when you open the account if there is a way around this fee.

Many time fees can be avoided by simply asking for no fee accounts or asking them to please waive fees for a while. We have had good success with this strategy. Financial institutions, however, make money when they charge you fees; therefore, fees are not going away. You have to learn your bank's system and try to work within it. If your bank seems too restrictive for your needs, then look for another. Never in history have Americans had so many banking choices.

There are two types of bank accounts. The first is a "single account" that you would normally open that provides you and you alone access to all the money inside the account. The second type of account is a joint account. If you are under 18 and you create a bank account, your parents must also be on the account and are also responsible for your actions—such as unpaid bills. If you create investment accounts, the same rule applies, and your parents do have ultimate control over those accounts.

Traditional married couples typically (but not always) create "joint accounts" that provide both people full access to their bank accounts. The growth of non-traditional couples, however, creates a growing need for more and more joint accounts of non-legally married couples. I urge everyone not to create a joint bank account with your romantic/domestic partner unless you know them well and you have both committed to a long-term relationship.

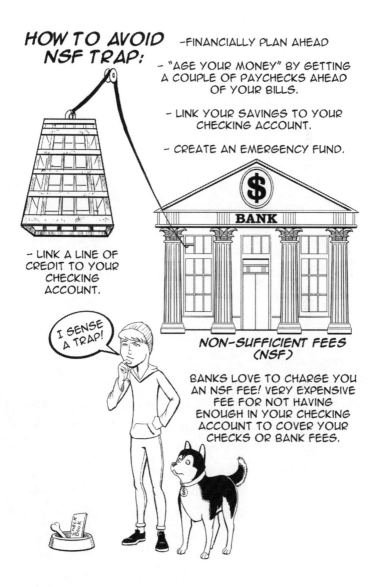

HOW TO AVOID NSF TRAP:

-FINANCIALLY PLAN AHEAD

- "AGE YOUR MONEY" BY GETTING A COUPLE OF PAYCHECKS AHEAD OF YOUR BILLS.

- LINK YOUR SAVINGS TO YOUR CHECKING ACCOUNT.

- CREATE AN EMERGENCY FUND.

BANK

- LINK A LINE OF CREDIT TO YOUR CHECKING ACCOUNT.

I SENSE A TRAP!

NON-SUFFICIENT FEES (NSF)

BANKS LOVE TO CHARGE YOU AN NSF FEE! VERY EXPENSIVE FEE FOR NOT HAVING ENOUGH IN YOUR CHECKING ACCOUNT TO COVER YOUR CHECKS OR BANK FEES.

Entering into a joint account automatically attaches financial and legal obligations to both parties. For example:

- Unintended Inheritance: Despite whatever wills or last instructions you might leave, a joint account means joint, legal ownership of the money inside those accounts.

- Unexpected Creditors: If your partner has creditors you don't know about, or they have forgotten about, you pick up varying legal and financial obligations to pay those debts from your joint account.

- Full Access: Your partner can withdraw all the funds any time they want. As a person who has been divorced twice early in life, I can tell you that even if you are married this can get tricky if the two of you ever split-up.

- Medical Eligibility: Joint accounts can also impact medical eligibility for certain medical insurance plans—as in you have too much money now to be eligible for certain insurance programs.

Sally (not her real name) graduated from college, obtained a great job, and was doing very well financially. She met an older guy and they began dating. Her relatively new boyfriend convinced Sally to open a joint bank account and combine their funds. Although the boyfriend had little money saved, Sally had accumulated $61K in savings over her lifetime. After the accounts were combined, the boyfriend withdrew all her money and left Sally broke. Her attempt to file fraud or theft charges against the boyfriend were rejected by the police and bank because it was a joint account, which gave the boyfriend equal ownership of Sally's funds. Although the funds might be able to be recovered in civil court (or at least part of the money), you easily see the problem of creating joint bank accounts with either close friends or potential romantic partners.

Cheat Codes:

You now understand the difference between financial institutions and the advantages and disadvantages each presents. We also now understand the most common fees banks charge you and how best to avoid. Just as importantly, you now understand the difference between single and joint accounts and the legal and financial obligations that come along with creating a joint account with a new romantic partner.

Up Next:

We can now concentrate on getting our minds right for budgeting. Budgeting is almost entirely a mental game. If you don't have the correct mindset and strategy, your efforts to control your spending and create financial abundance will fail miserably. A budget is one of the most important weapons in your Money Game!

Online Resource:

Learn more about mobile banking and other financial topics with this informational website: https://www.practicalmoneyskills.com/

9

The Budgeter's Mental Game

"All limits are self-imposed." — **Ernest Holmes**

The importance of your mindset is highlighted by the life story of Ernest Holmes. Ernest was born into poverty on January 21, 1887, on a small farm in Lincoln, Maine. Holmes became a writer, inventor, teacher and businessman. He is famous for writing The Science of Mind and other books on metaphysics. He also founded the international monthly periodical, Science of Mind Magazine, which is still being published today. One of his famous concepts is that our thoughts have power. Our thoughts create our experiences and control much of how we view and interact with our world. Quality thoughts create a quality life, while negative thoughts create negative results. He also believed that your life is a mirror and will naturally reflect your thoughts back to you; therefore, if you believe budgeting is a chore, burdensome, or a hardship, then that is the experience you will have. When Ernest Holmes died in 1960, his net worth was kept secret by his family and is currently unknown.

Budgeting is not only essential to your financial success, but equally vital to accomplishing your life's most treasured dreams. Your goals will not happen by magic; they happen by doing the work in the trenches to create the outcomes you desire.

Being a successful budgeter is all about having the correct mindset.

Not having the correct mindset—often overlooked by budgeting books and even by financial instructors—is the number-one reason why so many people fail at budgeting.[1]

A budget is a requirement because it prevents you from overspending the money you have available. Many people make a lot of money, but they have nothing left—or even a negative balance—at the end of the month. You don't have to be poor to live from paycheck to paycheck and sadly, having a large amount of debt can replicate this same condition.[2]

The wealthy outspend their budgets all the time. Unfortunately, highly paid athletes, lottery winners and celebrities go broke every day. This is especially true if they did not make their money over time or obtained sudden wealth, like a lottery winner. They did not develop the ground-level skills required to manage their money as their prosperity increased.

If you do not budget, you will overspend your income!

Overspending is addictive and sucks you into a downward momentum that will eventually create a negative impact upon every single aspect of your life. Overspending leads to:

- Financial regrets

- No savings
- Excessive debt
- Increased financial stress
- Lower self-esteem
- Poor life decisions
- Escalating life chaos
- Relationship stress with your significant other or a substantial roadblock to finding a romantic partner
- Failure to achieve your treasured goals and dreams

Overspending is amazingly easy to do. Even those of us who try to follow a budget sometimes struggle with it.

Budgeting is inevitable!

The old saying goes, "Nothing is certain in this world except death and taxes." Well, whoever made this up forgot to mention budgeting. You will either budget and create savings that will significantly improve all aspects of your life in the future, or you will budget and live frugally because you spent too much money and are now trying to stay afloat financially. One way or the other, budgeting is inevitable. Since that is the case, why not make living frugally count for something? Budgeting has the power to dramatically change your financial situation for the better in a short amount of time.

There will never be a time you can skip budgeting. Even millionaires budget if they wish to remain millionaires.

You did, after all, put considerable time, energy, and stress into creating your income! Your work should be honored and not destroyed by careless overspending. Budgeting will ensure that the work you did to earn your income counts for something today and in the future.

Jenny Carrol and her husband Jimmy from Cape Coral, Florida say that budgeting changed their lives. Jenny describes her challenging journey in her blog, "Women Who Money." Jenny explains that she and her husband were newly married when Jimmy was diagnosed with cancer. He is currently without evidence of disease now, but they were left in debt. The second part of the story had to do with fertility issues. They solved that problem with a clinic's help, but both medical difficulties left them $90K in debt. Together, they set a goal of becoming debt free in only twenty-four months. Amazingly, they succeeded. They accomplished this goal by increasing their incomes, budgeting and being frugal. Today, they are debt free, except for their mortgage. They have no car loans, student loans or any other kind of loan and are now working on their savings and investing goals.[3]

Common feelings associated with being on a budget include feeling unduly restricted, deprived of life's finer things or forced to live in near poverty. This mindset will not lead you to success. Ernest Holmes would likely agree that thinking in this manner will very likely produce poor budgetary outcomes. To be successful with long-term budgeting, you are going to have to get your head into the budgeting game. That means creating a mindset that will enable you to resist temptation and not feel constantly deprived of the things you want in life.

Below are three different mindsets that can help keep you motivated to work through the routine tasks related to your budgeting process. Pick one or more of these mindsets that works best for you.

The first mindset is called Me, Incorporated (which we will now shorten to Me, Inc.). Me, Inc. companies must produce a profit! If a corporation does not become profitable quickly, it will face a shutdown.

Did you know when all is said and done, individuals aren't much different from businesses?

People confront the same profit requirement that controls all businesses and, whether they understand it or not, are essentially a Me, Incorporated. At our house, we call it Faulkner, Incorporated. Just like any other business, you *cannot* go deeper and deeper into debt in your weekly, monthly, and quarterly budget reports and remain solvent. If you are operating in the red as an individual, you must quickly make changes to become profitable. The idea is to use a more logical and business-like approach to analyzing your personal budget. This technique's big advantage is that it provides the emotional distance required for individuals to calm themselves and their budget anxiety.

Just like any other business, Me, Inc. will have to analyze income and expense statements on a monthly, quarterly, and annual basis. Me, Inc. should also strive to increase profitability each year.

The idea is to use this business approach by examining the following:

- Do I make a profit each month (savings)?

- What changes can I make to become more profitable (more savings)?
- What is my largest expense category and how can I reduce it?
- What can I do without temporarily to increase my short-term profitability?
- How can I eliminate some less-important expenses to increase profits?
- How can I use my monthly profits to create even more profits (investing)?
- How can I increase my annual income?

Companies that break even or go slightly in the red are not considered good companies for investing. Make your Me, Inc. a powerhouse of financial strength. Looking at your budget from this perspective can empower you to keep working through the budgeting processes.

Brandon Copeland, previously mentioned in Chapter 3, is now entering his 8th NFL season. Copeland is a big fan of the Me, Inc. mindset and considers himself a business entity.[4]

Do you have the courage to live a different type of lifestyle than your peers? Success with budgeting has been found by those who cultivate a mindset of living their lives with intentionality. The idea is to align your daily actions with your goals and values so you can live your life filled with a sense of purpose and meaning.

GET YOUR MIND IN THE GAME! NOT HAVING THE CORRECT MINDSET IS THE #1 REASON BUDGETS FAIL!

MINDSET #1: "ME INC."

- CORPORATIONS MUST PRODUCE A PROFIT OR FACE SHUTDOWN.
- PEOPLE AREN'T REALLY ANY DIFFERENT FROM CORPORATIONS

- CREATE YOUR OWN "ME INC."
- ANALYZE YOUR INCOME & EXPENSES.

PROFIT = SAVINGS!

- HOW CAN I MAKE MORE PROFIT EACH MONTH?

- HOW CAN I INCREASE INCOME & REDUCE EXPENSES? MAKE YOUR "ME INC." A POWERHOUSE!

- CORPORATIONS THAT BREAK EVEN OR GO SLIGHTLY INTO DEBT ARE NOT GOOD COMPANIES.

In a study by UCLA, those who live with a sense of purpose are happier and more motivated to succeed.[5] Also, Harvard research has shown that those who have a sense of purpose with accompanying goals live longer and are in better health.[6]

In an intentional life, you decide each day if what you are doing (and spending) is consistent with achieving your goals, outcomes, and the life purpose you have chosen. If it is not consistent with your goals, you do not spend the money. With each expense you ask yourself, "Does this action move me forward toward my goals and purpose? Is spending this money consistent with those outcomes?" If not, you need to use your free will and adjust your actions to better reflect your chosen priorities. Living in this manner provides greater serenity, more motivation and clarifies your life's purpose.

Finally, consider cultivating a growth mindset to improve your budget performance. A growth mindset emphasizes continually expanding your mind and skills to achieve goals and outcomes you desire. People who focus on growth accomplish things they may have never believed possible for them.

For example, when I was in high school if someone had told me I would graduate from college with academic honors and earn a master's degree, I would not have believed it. I hated school with a passion, and I was not good at it. A little later in life, when I learned I had undiagnosed ADD that was making school very difficult for me, I developed techniques to overcome my attention deficit barriers. That growth within myself opened an entirely new world of opportunity for me. I learned to succeed in the academic settings, which later super charged my journey towards my goals.

All real growth occurs internally first and then it is manifested outwardly.

Usually, we are obsessed or even crippled by what we believe we can't do. For example, we might believe we aren't good with numbers and math, we might believe we aren't good with money, or we might even believe we just aren't smart enough to do well with our finances. These are simply mindsets you absorbed growing up but very likely are not actual limitations. Even if they are actual limitations, you can learn to overcome most limitations if you choose to do so.

#3 GROWTH MINDSET TO IMPROVE BUDGET & FINANCIAL PERFORMANCE

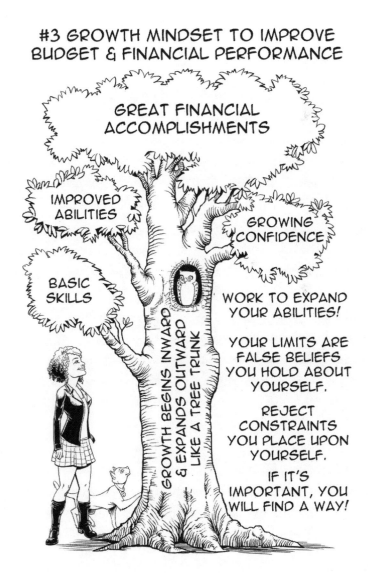

GREAT FINANCIAL ACCOMPLISHMENTS

IMPROVED ABILITIES

GROWING CONFIDENCE

BASIC SKILLS

GROWTH BEGINS INWARD & EXPANDS OUTWARD LIKE A TREE TRUNK

WORK TO EXPAND YOUR ABILITIES!

YOUR LIMITS ARE FALSE BELIEFS YOU HOLD ABOUT YOURSELF.

REJECT CONSTRAINTS YOU PLACE UPON YOURSELF.

IF IT'S IMPORTANT, YOU WILL FIND A WAY!

With a growth mindset, you understand that your limits are just false beliefs you hold about yourself. You consciously reject the constraints placed upon you by past experiences and upbringing. You utilize free will to make budgeting a priority in your life because it helps you accomplish your goals and improve your life, both in the present and in the future. If something is a priority, you will find a way to get it done.

Elon Must considers himself to be a person with a growth mindset and dedicates himself to constantly learning, growing, and improving his skills.[7]

Remember the Ernest Holmes quote at the beginning of the chapter says, "All limits are self-imposed?" Obviously, Holmes had a growth mindset that served him well throughout his career.

Cheat Codes:

This chapter is one of the keys to making your finances work for you rather than against you. The first thing to know is that budgeting is inevitable, and everyone must budget—even millionaires. Overspending is addictive and creates downward momentum that could be hard to reverse later. One of the most common reasons budgets fails is that the budgeter doesn't possess the correct mindset. The first of three good mindsets for budgeters is Me Incorporated, where the budgeter takes more of a business view of their finances. The second mindset is living with intention or intentionality, where you consciously choose to let your everyday actions support your overall goals. The final mindset for budgeters is growth, where you strive to improve your life, skills, abilities and outcomes every day.

Next Up:

Now that you have helpful mindsets to assist in becoming a successful budgeter, you can move on to creating an actual budget. Likely, you already have an idea of what a budget entails. Keep reading to understand the steps needed to live a rewarding life while controlling your spending.

Online Game:

One of the jobs of a Hollywood movie producer is budgeting the funds available to produce the best product. Try playing that role here: https://www.mimm.gov/

10

The Best Budget to Up Your Game Play

"An hour of planning can save you ten hours of doing."
— **Dale Carnegie**

Dale Carnegie helped pioneer the importance of planning in accomplishing goals. Carnegie was born into poverty on a Missouri farm in 1888. He went on to become one of the best-selling authors of all time, and an instructor and a pioneer in the field of success and confidence. Carnegie believed that all you need to do is set your intentions and plan your approach and you could overcome most problems—including the financial tasks of budgeting and saving. He seems to have been right, as he wrote several international bestselling books over his lifetime and his net worth at the time of his death was believed to have been $1.5 million.

Even with a very modest income stream, the first order of business is to create a budget. Most high school students don't have a full-time job, steady income, or regular bills when they graduate. All of these responsibilities are usually handled by parents or caregivers. The day after you graduate high school, however, this situation may abruptly end. Your financial situation will change whether you remain at home with your parents and they pay your bills, you go away to college, or you move into your own place and have a job to support this move.

> The Money Game is played on a time clock, and your time begins ticking away the moment you graduate—or even if you fail to graduate.[1]

How you use your time on your game clock matters. You are battling the forces of long-term inflation, rising taxes and the time it takes investing and compounding interest to create wealth on your behalf. Not that you shouldn't seek higher education or further training, but make sure the time spent doing it creates significant future value, so the rest of your game clock time counts for even more.

Also, failing to budget or just getting by financially is wasting time on your game clock; time spent without creating any helpful, forward financial momentum. If this thought causes you stress, take heart. No one is perfect and you are still young. You can overcome your past mistakes. My primary point is, however, that it would be way easier and much more fun if you began creating prosperity right away. Don't wait! Imagine the head start that would give you. Also, if you read this book, you will already know more than the vast majority of high school graduates, freshmen attending college, or even more than most college graduates.

Even if you don't understand yet why time matters, you should begin to learn the skills you need to make the most of today and tomorrow. The skill that will help you the most in the many years to come is budgeting. Budgeting is the most hated, yet vitally important financial skill you can have. Building a budget always begins with recording your income and listing every dollar you spend (expense or payment) for a couple of months. You can't build a budget unless you know your basic income and expense numbers. Don't be embarrassed or afraid of those numbers. Everyone must start somewhere.

Budget Overview:
You can build a budget for any time period. People typically complete monthly budgets, although I have seen some done on a weekly basis. Below is the basic idea of how a monthly budget works.

Monthly Budget:
Monthly Income - Monthly Fixed Expenses - Monthly Variable Expenses = Savings

The aim is to have some savings at the end of each month, quarter and at the end of the year. Savings will make your life easier. A lack of savings will make your life much more difficult and stressful. All the previous steps (or game levels) we have discussed are tailored to creating valuable savings.

> Savings equals greater strength and stamina
> as you play the Money Game.

Right now, you might feel that budgeting is about pinching pennies so hard your fingers bleed. I won't lie. The initial shock of changing your lifestyle may be rough for beginners. Here is something other personal finance books may not mention: If you stick with it, after a short time, budgeting is not really a big deal anymore.

Here's why:

- You will make more money as each year passes, giving you more funds with which to work.

- As you make more money, a larger percentage is available to fund occasional luxuries.

- You adjust to budgeting as a normal part of your life, and it no longer creates anxiety.

- In a few years, you will have paid down any debts that are holding you back, and even more income is freed up to fund your daily life.

- You can place most of your budgeting actions on automatic pilot (direct deposit of your paycheck and automatic payments from checking) so that you don't have to think about this chore most of the time.

- Many of your peers, who never bothered to budget, will soon have to deal with their debt and won't have funds available to do fun things, so you won't miss out.

- Successful budgeting increases your self-esteem, making you feel great about yourself and your success.

My Favorite Budget:

I am a proponent of utilizing the 50/30/20 budget. This particular budget was made popular by Elizabeth Warren in a 2005 book she coauthored with Amelia Warren Tyagi, *All Your Worth: The Ultimate Lifetime Money Plan.*[2]

What makes this budget so great is that the 20% savings category is an absolute priority in your budget. You route 20% of your pay into savings when you first get your paycheck (see Chapter 14) by direct deposit. What you do with your savings is very important as well, which we'll cover in Chapter 17.

BUDGETING EFFORT VS. MONEY

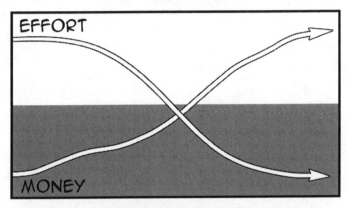

IF YOU CONTINUE TO BUDGET, MONEY INCREASES AND BUDGETING EFFORT DECREASES.

- YOU ADJUST TO BUDGETING AS A NORMAL PART OF LIFE.

- YOU MAKE MORE & MORE MONEY OVER TIME.

- YOU PAY OFF LOANS AND DEBTS QUICKER, GIVING YOU MORE MONEY FOR DAY-TO-DAY LIVING.

- YOU CAN AUTOMATE MOST ROUTINE BUDGET CHORES.

The 50/30/20 budget mix includes using 50% of your take-home pay to cover your needs, or regular monthly bills and expenses, for food, clothing, shelter, debt, and transportation. Then 30% goes toward your expenses in the "wants" category, which also covers rewards for living by your budget. Funds from your 30% "wants" category is used to go out and have fun or to purchase something outside your "needs" (50%) category. If you have trouble and go over your budget in some other category, you can pull funds from the reward category (a subcategory of "wants"). This helps create a self-correcting loop that makes you pay attention to your numbers and gives you an incentive to stay within your budget parameters. The 20% savings category is then routed into your savings and investing plan(s), ideally by direct deposit. That way, you don't ever see this money and have less chance of spending it rather than saving it. Twenty percent is the magic number that gives you the best chance of creating real prosperity over time.

Summary of the 50/30/20 Budget Categories:

50% = NEEDS
Housing, utilities, car, insurance—basically, expenses you cannot function without

30% = WANTS
Items you want to buy or activities you like to do—going on a date, going to the movies with friends or having a meal out

20% = SAVINGS
Money you place into either a savings account or some type of investment

Some subcategories such as gas or food could fall within the Wants or Needs categories. They can go in either or you can break them up into required vs extra. It's up to you.

A Detailed Example of a 50/30/20 Budget:

It is impossible to include every possible category, but this will give you a good idea of which expense goes under each category. Remember, recording your spending for a few months illustrates exactly what categories you need in your budget.

Income: List all income you normally receive each month.

- Wages from Job 1
- Wages from Job 2

The 50% Needs Category:

- Rent
- Insurance: Car
- Insurance: Renter's
- Loan Payments
- Electric
- Water
- Trash
- Internet
- Phone
- Basic grooming (hair cut)
- Student Loan Payment
- Vehicle Maintenance
- Groceries
- Work Clothes
- Gas

The 30% Wants Category:

- Reward for following your budget
- Eating Out

- Entertainment
- Hobbies
- Coffee from a coffee shop (rather than coffee from home)
- Streaming Service (Netflix/Hulu/Spotify)
- Vehicle Improvements (anything beyond basic repairs)
- Specialty Groceries (any items beyond basics)
- Grooming (hair enhancements/color, waxing, threading, manicure, tanning, beard/mustache sculpting)
- Babysitting (any time not required for work)
- Gas (other than required to go to work)
- Special Clothing Items

The 20% Savings Category:

- Savings Account
- Emergency Fund
- Investing Accounts

Simplified Example of 50/30/20 Monthly Budget:

Due Date		Amount	Total
	Income From Job	$3,500	
	Income from a business/ side gig*	$500	
	Total Income:		$4,000
	Expenses (Needs):		
1	Housing	$1,100	

Larry Faulkner

Due Date		Amount	Total
5	Gas/Electric	$50	
5	Water	$25	
10	Trash	$35	
15	Transportation (bus, ride sharing, car payment)	$500	
20	Auto Insurance	$50	
25	Credit Card Minimum Payment	$30	
(varies)	Groceries	$210	
	Subtotal Expenses (Needs):		**$2,000**
	Expenses (Wants):		
	Going Out with Friends or Date Night	$490	
	Fast Food	$200	
	Gas	$150	
	Coffee/Latte & Snack	$60	
	Lunch at Work	$300	
	Subtotal Expenses (Wants):		$1,200
	Total Expenses (Needs + Wants): $2,000 + $1,200 =		$3,200
	Income - Bills: $4,000 - $3,200 =		**$800 (Savings)**

Determining amounts per category for $4,000 in income using a 50/30/20 budget:

- 50% of income for needs expenses ($4,000 x .50) = $2,000

- 30% of income for wants expenses ($4,000 x .30) = $1,200
- 20% of income for savings ($4,000 x .20) = $800

Of course, there are plenty of people who hate a 50/30/20 budget and plenty of people who say it can't be done! I can tell you from personal experience, however, we not only saved 20% of our income, but we eventually worked up to saving 50% of our income.

"People who say it cannot be done should not interrupt those who are doing it." — **George Bernard Shaw**

An Irish writer who wrote over sixty British plays during his career. Shaw eventually won the Nobel Prize in Literature in 1926. He was the first person to ever win that award and an Academy Award (Best Adapted Screenplay to Film) in the same year.

Whatever ratios you decide upon, a budget at its very core is all about making decisions. If going out on Saturday night with your friends or on a date is super important to you, then cool! You just have to adjust your spending and cut out less-important areas of spending in the "wants" category. The purpose of a budget is to acquire the data necessary to make informed decisions, so you are able to do the things that are important to you while still hitting your savings goals.

Once you complete your budget, it is likely set for a while, and you only need to follow it. As circumstances change, however, your budget must also change. If your income goes up or down, all the above categories will likely need to be adjusted. If you should suddenly incur an unexpected expense (e.g., medical procedure) that you will need to pay over time, this will also cause budget adjustments. Also, rapid inflation in the economy, meaning goods and services cost more (like in 2022), may require adjusting your budget.

If you're the type of person who stresses out over creating a budget, even after considering the helpful budgeting mindsets in the previous chapter, there are some reasonably good work-arounds you can use. You can try mapping your budget. This shift in thinking uses creativity and can help you overcome budget anxiety. You create a chart with a box labeled Income at the top of the map flowing downward to a box labeled Life. On the left side of the Income box, list items from the 50% Needs category. On the right side of the box, list items from your 30% Wants category. Both sets of expenses flow into the Life box along with your income. Your hard-earned savings drop from the bottom of the Life box. Be creative with it and draw small pictures in the expenses and income categories. Activating your creative brain can distract you from your budgeting anxiety.

Another strategy is to only work on your budget for about fifteen minutes each day. This method can reduce any feelings of dread and apprehension.

Jamie Griffin says he knew he was in debt but wasn't really all that concerned about it until he fell in love and got married. After the wedding, he and his new wife realized they had a whopping $90K in student debt between them. The silver lining was that he and his wife learned how to budget their income from the first day of their marriage. In five years, using a disciplined budget, they became debt free. Budgeting can absolutely change your life for the better.[3]

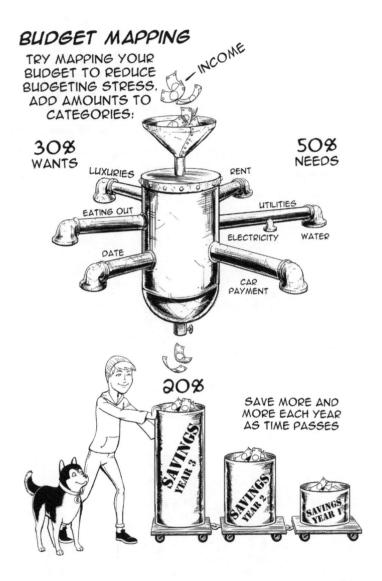

The final strategy to overcome budget anxiety or avoidance is looking at your budget as a spending plan—not a restrictive document. Sometimes this changes your perception and thinking enough, that it allows you to move forward. After all, developing a plan is how you get the most out of the money you have available.

Cheat Codes:

To review, a budget helps you gain control of both your money and your life. Without a budget, everything is done on the fly, which creates chaos, excess spending, and wastes time on your game clock that you could be using to build prosperity and upward momentum. Failing to budget also deprives you of the opportunity to make decisions about how your money should be spent to bring you the most benefit. If you stress out about budgeting, you can try mapping your budget by turning it into a diagram type drawing. You can also limit the amount of time each day you work on your budget to keep your stress low. Finally, you can reframe your thinking and consider a budget as a spending plan rather than a restrictive document.

Up Next:

We need to talk about the game's deadliest trap—too much debt! The controlled use of debt is important to your financial well-being and affects your ability to live the life you want in the future.

Online Resources:

This game, with levels from high school through college, teaches you about budgeting your income and has tests to see where you stand: https://www.claimyourfuture.org/play/

11

Avoid the Game's Deadly Hidden Trap

"Knowledge makes a man unfit to be a slave."
— **Fredrick Douglass**

Famous human rights advocate, anti-slavery activist, and political ally of President Lincoln, Fredrick Douglass was born into slavery in 1818 in Maryland. He soon saw that freedom was linked to knowledge, so he educated himself in secret. Slaves educating themselves was considered a crime in slave states. He escaped to freedom in 1838 by disguising himself as a sailor and purchasing a train ticket to New York. The journey occurred without incident, and he was free upon reaching his destination. Douglass found a job and began speaking and writing about his experiences as a slave. He was a transformational figure during the critical period leading up to the Civil War as America rose-up and rejected slavery as an institution. At the time of his death, he had a net worth of $50 thousand (approximately $1.15 million in today's money).

Those who have developed financial knowledge know they should avoid consumer debt. Take the case of Holly Carey for example. Carey had $55K in debt and after reading a personal finance book, she was able to use the information to develop a plan and take action to improve her financial life. Twenty-six months later, she was able to free herself from her debt.[1]

> Debt at the consumer level is extremely damaging to both your happiness and life satisfaction![2]

Do-over are always possible, especially since most readers are young, but too much debt can easily turn into a game fail. Debt can turn you into a virtual slave to your creditors and drain away all your time and energy servicing (paying) those debts. You would be in a better position if you could spend your time creating prosperity and winning your own Money Game.

Throughout time, a clear link between debt and slavery has been well documented. For example, in ancient times, people sometimes sold themselves into slavery to pay their debts or were forcibly taken as a slave due to their unpaid obligations.

America also has a history of indebted servitude, even though it goes under different names. Indentured servants were brought over from other countries and, in exchange for their passage, they pledged to work for the landowners for a certain number of years. They were typically directed to farm a landowner's estate. Later, when this practice and outright slavery were outlawed, the widespread use of sharecropping came into fashion. Sharecropping involves a resident farmer growing crops on someone else's land. In exchange, the farmer obtains a meager share of the crop's proceeds. Somehow, the farmer was always either indebted to the landowner or made just enough money to survive.

Peonage is a Spanish term for workers who were indebted to a mining company for supplies, a place to live and transportation to the camp. They were given wages that were less than, or just barely covered, their expenses.

In the 21st century, Americans seem almost eager to put themselves into significant debt to purchase consumer and luxury items. If left unchecked, this behavior eventually creates a type of debt servitude. However, the U.S. does not have the worst debt-to-income culture. Japan, Korea, Switzerland, and the Netherlands have the highest debt-to-household income ratios in the world.

Although imprisonment for debts was outlawed in America in 1833, you could still end up arrested over a debt should the right set of circumstances occur. For example, take the case of Rhonda who resides in Maryland. Rhonda had a minor traffic accident. The police arrived and completed a routine accident report. A standard record check by the police, however, revealed a warrant for Rhonda's arrest and she was subsequently taken into custody. Rhonda had an unpaid debt from an old gym membership. She had been ordered into court on a civil proceeding because of her gym membership debt. She didn't attend the hearing because she didn't have any money at the time and just considered the entire matter a nuisance. Unfortunately, failing to appear when ordered into court could (and does in most states) result in a warrant being issued for your arrest.[3] This is just an example of how things can escalate out of control if debt is not dealt with in a timely manner. Other debts for which you could be arrested include unpaid taxes you have been ordered to pay and various court-ordered fines—such as traffic citations.

As I mentioned in Chapter Three, as people age and look back over their lives a very common regret was spending money they had not yet earned.[4] Unfortunately, this is an extremely common practice in America, and 75% of us admit we carry high-interest debt on our credit cards from one month to the next (average balance of $5,315).[5] Of course, credit cards are only the tip of this iceberg. Other common debts people carry from month to month include:

- Personal loans
- Auto loans
- Mortgages
- College loans

Any one of these debts can become so large it can take over your entire life. All the debts together can consume your entire paycheck and leave you with less than nothing on payday. In the debt trap, you sell your future labor to purchase items you may or may not need today, which is essentially indentured servitude. You become unable to pursue your goals because you are constantly servicing (paying) your large debt(s). This situation traps you in jobs, in relationships, in certain communities or in situations you could come to resent over time. You cannot make the desired changes to your life because you must make payments on your large debt. This is true of the poor, the middle class and even people who make a very large salary.

> The debt we find ourselves in occurs, at least in part, because of society's expectations of us.

For example, consider the consequences of paying for college, a large wedding, a home to start a family, a new car, and/or college for at least one child. These expectations can put you in a very dangerous situation if you are not careful.

Being trapped by debt is especially dangerous since it is riddled with financial risk. In the blink of an eye, you could lose your job due to an accident, the company could close down, or you could lose your job through corporate restructuring. Once unemployed and without significant savings, paying large bills becomes impossible.

THE DEBT WE FIND OURSELVES IN OCCURS, IN PART, DUE TO SOCIETY'S EXPECTATIONS OF US!

EXAMPLES
-COLLEGE DEBT
-BIG HOUSE
-GET MARRIED
-HAVE KIDS

☆ THINK FOR YOURSELF! ☆
WHAT DO YOU WANT?
WHAT ARE YOU WILLING TO PAY FOR?

HAVE KIDS
WEDDING
BUY A HOUSE
NEW CAR
COLLEGE FOR KIDS
PROM

CAT HAS A FORCE FIELD THAT BOUNCES AWAY SOCIETAL DEMANDS

DON'T FIGHT DOG
BE A GOOD KITTY
DON'T CLAW COUCH

CATS DON'T CARE WHAT SOCIETY THINKS. BE THE CAT!

Debt and loan factors that increase your financial risk:

- Long loan payment period (think student loans or long-term home mortgages)
- Large monthly payment
- Large amount borrowed
- High loan interest rate (a 3% interest rate is less risky than an 8% interest rate).
- Several outstanding loans
- No savings

Some people now feel the newest form of indentured servitude comes from student loan debt.

That may sound a little extreme, but I can show you why it is not such a radical opinion. You can easily work your whole life to pay off student loans! The drain on your income can kill whatever chance you might have to ever create prosperity because it can suck away all your extra money. Instead of filling your investment accounts, you are filling a lender's investment account. You barely scrape by, while lenders handsomely profit. Yet schools, educational counselors, uninformed parents, and society constantly push student loans to America's young adults. Why do they do this? Either they are clueless about these loan terms, they are motivated by social pressures, or they stand to profit somehow. Also, it could be a simple matter of counselors being employed by the education sector and are representing the education industry in their meetings with high school students.

CREDIT RISKS

TOTAL AMOUNT OWED ON LOAN — High / Low

LOAN REPAYMENT PERIOD — Long / Short

MONTHLY PAYMENT AMOUNT — Large / Small

INTEREST RATE — High / Low

TOTAL NUMBER OF LOANS — Many / 0

SAVINGS — 0 / Large

CREDIT RISK METER

"...did you know student loan debt is the most dangerous debt any of us can have?" — Suze Orman, author, columnist, investor, producer, and activist for financial literacy for women with a net worth of over $75 million.

Student loans must be paid. Even filing bankruptcy will typically not cancel your obligation to pay the loan(s). Nonpayment can create penalties that are as much as 18% of the total loan.

If you don't make your student loan payments, any professional license you've earned could be suspended and you won't be able to work in your field. Your driver's license can also be suspended and any federal tax refunds you might be expecting could be seized until your loans are paid.

That's not all! Your Social Security payments could be seized to satisfy your school debt if you fail to pay it before you are elderly. If your parents cosigned for your loan, the lender may go after your parents for your payments. Even if you die, private student loans will likely be passed on to your parents if they co-signed for your loans.

This type of loan has the force of law behind it, and it can crush you underneath its legal and civil weight. Almost 50% of all millennials feel that finances entirely control their lives, and they are doing very poorly financially. More than 30% of all Americans feel controlled by their money- "they will never have enough money to get what they want in life."[6] Of course you can pay your debt off if you set goals, create a plan, and relentlessly work your plan to achieve your goals.

Phil (twenty-seven years old) moved into his dad's basement after college and lived there rent free. In exchange, he babysat his younger stepbrother and did numerous chores around his dad's house when he was off work. He lived on an amazingly low budget of $500 a month. He used the rest of his monthly salary of $3,000 to pay his college loans.[7]

I commend Phil for his ability to set and achieve worthy financial goals but imagine if Phil had lived at home to begin his college career and paid his way as he went. All the money he saved after graduation could have been put toward creating wealth and securing a future filled with prosperity. So, I say again, student loans are part of a modern debt-driven system of indentured servitude. In fact, smart young people compare the return on investment of a degree vs. the anticipated income in their chosen field. As of 2023:

- In-state students attending and staying at a public four-year college will expect to pay, on average, $25,707 for a single academic year.
- Students attending and staying at a private four-year university, on average, can expect to pay a total of $54,501 per academic year.[8]

Compare the above costs with salary ranges for your preferred career. Search the Bureau of Labor Statistics: https://www.bls.gov/oes/current/oes_nat.htm

Now, if you feel your life's purpose is to become a social worker (typically paid a lower wage compared to a very expensive degree), I totally get it. After all, who am I to tell you not to pursue your dream job? I will say, however, the smart thing here might be to deviate from the traditional path and reimagine how you might obtain your social work degree. Can you obtain grants for working in low-income areas, can you get scholarships, or perhaps can you attend college part-time while working? Even if your parents are willing to pay for the degree, please think twice about how much you are asking them to spend and if it is the best use of their money.

It is not just the straight-up cost of college that becomes painful. The interest payments can, and frequently do, far exceed the initial cost of college if the loan is paid back over time. It all depends on the interest rate, fees charged, repayment period, and of course the amount you borrowed. Not understanding all these factors is a common path to indentured servitude.

If you so choose, there is a solid alternative to college. Skilled labor and the construction trades face one of the greatest shortages in modern times, with three to four million jobs available.[9] At least part of the problem is that guidance counselors and educators like to put high school graduates onto an assembly line that leads straight to college. At the same time, they provide little to no information about the possible benefits of pursing a specialized skilled trade or training certification. Unless high school students have exposure to the trades at home, they hear very little about this option at school.

Although certainly not a good fit for everyone, the skilled trades offer a terrific opportunity for those who want to work with their hands and minds in unison. With specialized skill and training, this group of high school graduates can quickly create an income level that few college graduates can equal for many years to come—if ever.

Learning a trade at a community college is a very good option, which can give you a trade certification and a two-year associate degree together in many cases. This can be the best of both worlds and may put you in a good position to finish your college degree later while attending part time. You don't have to go through the degree program, however, to obtain a trade or vocational certification. You can become certified reasonably quickly in something similar to a six-week certificate—depending upon the skill sets and certification you are looking to obtain. As education and training goes, the value of these certifications is well worth the effort, and they are an excellent return on investment in most cases. As an example, these certification programs are offered by the local Austin Community College in Texas:

- Accounting
- Computer Information Technology
- Fashion Design
- Marketing
- Real Estate
- Auto Mechanic

Certification programs can be found at a wide variety of high-quality outlets. Here are a few ideas to get you thinking and searching in areas that interest you:

Certifications are available, very cost effectively at coursera. org. Coursera has a strategic partnership with Google and IBM, as well as several academic universities like Stanford, Duke, Michigan, Penn State and many more. Their goal is to train future workers to be able to take jobs in partnering companies and in other organizations.[10] Examples of companies that partner with coursera.org:

- Google Data Analytics
- IBM Data Science
- IBM Data Analyst
- Digital marketing and e-commerce companies
- IT support companies
- Data analytics companies
- Project management companies
- Computer programming companies
- UX design companies (designing systems to be user friendly)

Other great sources include the adult career academy in your community. These career or technology academies generally offer a variety of skilled trade job certifications:

- Welding
- Carpentry
- Masonry
- Construction
- HVAC
- Pharmacy Technician
- Medical Scribe
- Phlebotomist
- Radiology Tech

If you can't afford a certification program, consider working in an apprentice program. Many apprentice programs begin paying you right away while you both work and learn. More than 90% of those who complete the apprentice program are hired by that company.[11] Visit apprenticeship.gov to find apprenticeship programs in your area or region.

Some people are not interested in what they consider to be a labor career (masonry for example). Other options include business, government, environmental and vocational skills. The number of possible certificates is nearly endless.

The annual average wage for a college-educated worker in the United States is $53,490 per year or $1,028 per week (U.S. Bureau of Labor Statistics). At the same time, they report the average salary for an electrician and plumber is over $63,000. The average salary for a carpenter is over $55,000. Not to be outdone, a truck driver makes around $55,000.[12] Now, consider that the cost of a trade or vocational school is one-third or less of the cost of a four-year college.

Did you know plenty of barbers become rich? Many barbers, after gaining experience, are able to generate six figures annually—which only happens to those who set goals and work to achieve them. Of course, what you do with your money also matters. The most striking example is barber Ramesh Babu, who was born into poverty in India. Ramesh's father was a barber, but died when Ramesh was very young, which left his mother and his siblings in poverty. His mother became a household servant to pay some basic bills. As a small child, Ramesh began taking odd jobs to make money to help her.

Later, Ramesh became a successful barber. At one point he purchased a new Mercedes. Ramesh worked so much in his barbershop, however, he never had time to drive his new car. He got the idea of renting it out when he wasn't using it. The idea blew up in popularity and everyone wanted to rent his Mercedes. Since India was becoming more prosperous and tourism was on the rise, he came up with idea of buying several Mercedes and renting them out. The business kept growing until Ramesh became the world's first billionaire barber. Now he rents his vehicles through his business Ramesh Tours and Travels. Even as a billionaire, Ramesh works in his shop as a barber for at least part of his day.[13]

Be leery of for-profit higher education institutions because they have a terrible reputation for failing to deliver the degree or certification while leaving you with huge debt. For example, students at ITT Technical College and Corinthian University had their loan payments cancelled by the federal government because ITT and Corinthian defrauded the federal government.[14] Experts strongly recommend you use a community college to obtain either the two-year degree or use the college's certification program.

You can always check your local community colleges' and the trade schools' recognition and accreditation at the Database of Accredited Postsecondary Institutions and Programs, at the

U.S. Department of Education ope.ed.gov/dapip/, or call them at 1-885-831-9922.[15]

DISCONNECT STUDENT DEBT
FROM FORMAL EDUCATION

SMARTYPANTS U

USE LOWER COST
METHODS OF
ATTENDING COLLEGE,
SUCH AS COMMUNITY
COLLEGE, PART-TIME
ATTENDANCE AND
TUITION
REIMBURSEMENT
OPPORTUNITIES
FROM AN EMPLOYER.

Cheat Codes:

America has a long history of indentured servitude, e.g., when a person sells all their future labor for money in the present. Americans seem to have a debt problem. Although we are not the worst debt-to-income nation, we definitely make the top ten list.

Many people believe modern-debt servitude flows from the skyrocketing cost of a college degree. A degree was once considered the fast track to financial abundance, now degree costs are so high that the return from the chosen field's salary must be weighed against the cost of a degree in that field. Frequently, you can get education for comparatively low costs by attending a two-year college first and then transferring to a cost-effective state college.

More and more people are skipping the degree, at least at first, and obtaining a training certification that allows them to start working right away, avoiding high debt. A career certification is not a barrier to building wealth. Be very careful, however, with for-profit schools for degrees or training certifications. Some of these institutions have a horrible reputation for high prices while having a long history of failing to deliver the degree.

Up Next:

Did you think you were done with report cards once you left high school or college? Unfortunately, you are not done with them. Now, credit bureaus report on your progress. A bad credit report can negatively impact many important aspects of your life. Read the next chapter to learn more about credit reports.

Online Game:

To experience money management and avoid debt, play Misadventures in Money Management: https://www.consumerfinance.gov/consumer-tools/educator-tools/servicemembers/mimm/

12

The Money Game's Report Card

"Do something today your future self will thank you for!"
— **Patrick Flanery**

Patrick Flanery *strongly believed a person should go out and create the future they desire. He was born in California in 1974 but raised on the farmland plains of Omaha, Nebraska. He is the author of the award-winning book Absolution about the shocking violence in South Africa. He is a professor of creative writing at the University of Reading, a columnist and is living in the UK. Flanery believes you must begin to shape your present to obtain the future you want. You can't wait around for the right conditions to naturally occur as they likely will never occur. His advice especially applies to personal finances as well credit score or credit worthiness. Flanery evidently followed his own advice as his net worth is rumored to be around $4 million.[1]*

If you thought you were done with report cards when you graduated high school, unfortunately, that is not quite the case. The Money Game has an ongoing report card from the credit bureaus that monitors all the details of your loans and payment history. Credit bureaus are companies that publish reports on your credit worthiness (the risk you represent to those who would loan you money) to future lenders. You cannot opt out of this report on your finances. Anytime you apply for a loan, the first thing a lender will do is obtain your credit report to see if you are a good risk or if they are likely to have trouble collecting their money from you.

You might recall that I've recommended you avoid most consumer credit. However, a certain amount of credit usage is necessary for modern life in order to generate a good credit report and score.

The credit bureaus or credit agencies that produce credit reports are government-sanctioned, private businesses and are not actually official government bureaus. Almost universally, companies that lend you money report your payment history to credit bureaus. Even your monthly utility company reports your payment history to these agencies. They also provide all the information you offered when you filled out your credit application to borrow money, get your utilities turned on or rent an apartment. The credit bureaus also research your past loan history, payment history and your income to determine your loan suitability. Based on this information, the credit bureaus produce your credit reports.

The primary credit bureaus in the U.S. include:

a. Experian

b. Equifax

c. TransUnion

d. Innovis (up-and-coming credit bureau)

The credit bureaus use a computer program developed by the Fair Isaac Corporation to produce a numerical score called a FICO score. The Fair Isaac Corporation is a data analysis, actuarial (see glossary) and software company. Your information is put into their special, super-secret computer formula, and your score is produced. The actual formula to obtain your score remains a closely guarded secret, so they can charge credit bureaus a licensing fee to use their software.

Your FICO score is supposed to roughly be based on the following:

- Payment history: 35%
- How much you owe: 30%
- Age of your payment history:15%
- The number of credit inquiries: 10%. Several inquiries could imply you are attempting to obtain various loans at once, which makes you a greater credit risk. Additionally, they begin to suspect fraudulent motives if the trend continues. If numerous inquiries begin to occur, they may systematically begin lowering your credit score.
- Types of credit you currently have: 10% (home loan, school loan, secured loan, etc.)

Credit Score Ranges and Meanings:

- 0 = No Credit Score
- 579 & Under = Poor Credit Score
- 580 - 669 = Fair Credit Score
- 670 - 739 = Good Credit Score
- 740 & Above = Very Good or Excellent Credit Score

FICO CREDIT SCORES & WHAT THEY MEAN

FICO: FAIR ISACC CORP. A DATA ACTUARIAL COMPANY DEVELOPED A SECRET FORMULA CREDIT BUREAUS NOW USE!

NO SCORE	POOR	FAIR	GOOD	GREAT
0	579 & LOWER	580 TO 669	670 TO 739	740 & ABOVE

Your debt in relation to your income—also known as debt-to-income (DTI) ratio is also relevant. All your debt (consumer loans, credit cards, car, personal loans, etc.) should be equal to or less than 36% of your monthly pay. So, if you have $1,300 in monthly debt payments that you pay from your $4,064 in monthly salary, you can calculate your DTI ratio by using this formula:

Take your total debt (all monthly debt payments added together) divided by monthly take-home pay. This will equal your percentage of debt (after you multiply the answer by 100 to turn it into a percentage). Don't get nervous about the math. Just grab your phone calculator and follow along:

- DTI = (all monthly debt payments divided by monthly pay) x 100
- Our example: $1,300 / $4,064 = .32
- .32 x 100 = 32%
- In our example, 32 % of the monthly take-home salary is the DTI.

When you get close to the 32% mark, credit bureaus will begin giving you a lower credit score for future loans. At 36%, your credit score will be poor. The actual formula uses gross pay, but I always calculate this percentage using net pay (take-home pay) instead to give myself some extra room. I suggest that you use the same method.

It would be very tempting at this point to simply ignore this whole mess. Don't even worry about your credit score since you plan on utilizing very little credit anyway. I wish we could think that way, but unfortunately, the Money Game we are all forced to play does not allow this strategy. Your credit score will be very important to you in the near future for the following reasons:

- **Emergencies:** Your ability to handle emergencies such as your car breaking down, a flat tire or a busted water heater in your home could require good credit. Otherwise, you must have cash on hand to handle every problem.

- **Job:** What kind of job you can obtain will likely be impacted by your credit report. Before an employer hires you, they typically perform a background check as well as a drug test, credit report and criminal record check. If you have bad credit, many employers will not hire you. They assume that if you don't pay attention to your bills, you are not likely to pay attention to the job they give you. This may be flawed logic, but it is part of the hiring process for many companies. Bad credit also makes you ineligible for many government positions. Some employers, including police departments and federal agencies that require security clearances, will even fire or pursue job-related discipline against you should you have bad credit or be reported for nonpayment. If you join the armed forces, they limit the kind of jobs available to those with bad credit. An interesting side note: Jobs are not limited for those who join the armed services out of high school with no credit!

- **Cash Flow:** Credit can temporarily help you if you have cash flow problems and you exercise discipline and pay it off immediately.

- **Large Purchases:** Bad credit makes it harder to complete large purchases such as appliances, a car, or even new tires for your car. Without credit, you must always have the cash on hand. In some cases, when you pay with cash, you must obtain a certified check and wait for the check to clear the bank before a store or dealership will let you take the product. Large amounts of cash ($10K or more) will draw scrutiny from the IRS and various law enforcement agencies who will likely assume the worst and investigate the money's origin. Businesses or private individuals are required by law to report to the IRS any purchase where cash is used in a trade or business payment of more than $10,000 in a single transaction or related transactions. [2]

- **Car Insurance Rates:** Those who have good credit typically get better car insurance rates. Statistics show those with good credit have better driving records. Whether or not this is actually the case, car insurance companies operate within this premise.

- **Housing Insurance Rates:** How much you pay for housing or renters' insurance is also impacted by your credit score. Insurance companies charge customers more if they believe they may have trouble obtaining payments or they believe customers are less responsible.

- **Cell Phone:** Your monthly cell phone rate is more expensive if you have bad credit, or a monthly rate is simply not available to those with poor credit. You will be stuck with a pre-paid plan for your cell phone.

- **Banking/Checking:** Banks may charge you more money in monthly service fees if you have bad credit. They just assume they will have trouble with your account.

- **No Credit:** What if you have no credit because you have never borrowed money? Having no credit is not quite as bad as poor credit. It may limit the places you can live, however, because landlords will be hesitant to rent to you. If you are just out of high school, it is expected that you will have no credit, and this may not be viewed quite as negatively. If you are older (college or college graduate) and have no credit score, it tends to be a red flag for fraud and will make landlords think twice about you.

A young man I know (we'll call him John) had sought to be a musician after high school. John had gone to California and played with a band for about a year. Although it was a great adventure and he learned a lot about life, financially this move was an utter disaster. Upon his return his family's home in Ohio, he started on the next chapter of his life.

John had success with a steady job in Ohio and was paying down his debts. Soon, however, he decided to join the Army and purse a career in the military, which would then allow him to use the GI bill when he got out of the Army and attend college for nearly free. In the interim, he could also create a career and develop expertise within his chosen field.

John got with a recruiter and was in the process of signing up in his career field (Intelligence) when he was surprisingly rejected for his first career choice. The security clearance required for this position would not accept someone with his poor credit score. Having no credit score was fine with the military but having a poor one disqualified people from this field.

John was stuck with his second choice—or so it seemed at the time. Everything did work out and John was able to attend college after a military tour, but he still remembers the sting of being rejected for a bad credit score. He vowed to never allow that to happen again. John is now doing extremely well financially and has a great credit score.

The good news is that if you can obtain a good credit score, you are able to level up in the Money Game and unlock special abilities. For example, a good score allows you to access lower interest rate loans, special offers only available to those with good credit and better monthly rates on a variety of common services. Obviously, you need a good credit score to help win your Money Game.

HOW TO MAINTAIN A GOOD CREDIT SCORE:

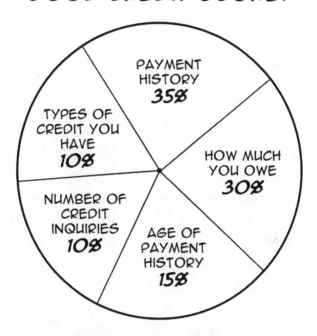

THESE ELEMENTS CREATE
YOUR CREDIT SCORE.

WORK ON MAKING TIMELY
PAYMENTS & KEEP YOUR
OVERALL CREDIT USAGE LOW.

How can a recent high school graduate get this done? Below are three methods to build a credit score that will help rather than hinder your money game:

1. **Obtain a prepaid credit card.** If a prepaid credit card has a $1,000 limit, that means you give the credit card company $1,000 up front, which they will hold as collateral. You then make purchases and payments just like a normal credit card. It does not say "prepaid" anywhere on the card, and no one knows it but you. If you make timely payments and keep a low balance, this builds your credit. A poor payment history will give you a very low score.

2. **Become an authorized user on your parents' card.** Of course, this means you owe your parents money each month for any purchases you make, which can get dicey if you don't meet your monthly obligation. Your parents take a risk by adding you as a user on their card as they know they (not you) will ultimately be held responsible should you not make payments or make late payments on your purchases.

3. **Ask your parents to cosign a loan for a vehicle.** You are responsible for this loan. If you make a late payment, however, your parents/cosigner will be notified, and nasty letters will go out to everyone on the loan. This might be a good way to keep you on track with payments, but it may also bring family strife if you make mistakes—intentional or otherwise. If you fail to pay your car loan, your parents will be forced to handle the loan themselves and it will damage everyone's credit. I have seen this seriously harm family relationships. So should you decide to use this strategy, make timely payments a priority.

3 STRATEGIES TO CREATE CREDIT IN YOUR NAME.

WARNING:
NOT MAKING PAYMENTS WILL DAMAGE YOUR FAMILY RELATIONSHIPS IF YOUR FAMILY COSIGNS LOANS FOR YOU.

As you can see, poor credit means you are charged more for loans and denied opportunities those with good credit will be able to access. An entire economic ecosystem exists to take advantage of people with poor credit ratings, little financial resources or younger consumers who don't yet understand the loan system. These loans range from payday loans, buy-now, pay-later loans, rent-to-own loans, and buy here/pay here loans with interest rates so high they would be illegal under normal circumstances. In fact, these types of loans are not covered under the normal consumer protection laws. In other words, these businesses feed on desperation and ignorance. Companies are increasing these types of loans (like Amazon for example) since people buy more items if they can pay for it later—a fact young consumers have not caught on to quite yet.

The most common way to create a poor credit score includes inadequate follow-through on your bills—late payments, forgotten payments or skipping payments until the next month. At the beginning of 2023, 33% of the "buy-now, pay-later loans" were in delinquency due to missed or late payments. Companies count on missed or late payments because they generate very large penalties and higher interest rates that kick-in—which creates extra profit for the lender.

The next most common way credit ratings are damaged is allowing your debt-to-income ratio (DTI) to become so high that creditors begin to restrict loan access.

What if you already have poor credit? You can fix it with a little effort and time. Improve your credit score with these steps:

1. Make your payments on time this month and every month after this.

2. Pay down and eliminate your debt to reduce your DTI ratio.

3. Deal with debts that have gone to collection agencies with either a payment plan or a one-time larger payment. Sometimes, if you have some money accumulated, a creditor will take a smaller amount to settle a bill and will mark it as paid in full. Just be sure you have any agreement

you negotiate in writing before you pay it, otherwise you could be caught off guard when a credit collection agency refuses to honor the deal later—which they are famous for doing.

4. Depending on the state in which you live, credit reporting agencies can only consider reports from debts that have not passed the state's time limits. Each state has its own rules and laws that forbid reporting on outstanding debts that have surpassed their legal time frames, which can range from three to seven years before a debt can be removed from your credit report or legal action can be pursued for collection purposes. After that, a debt can no longer be reported as outstanding on your credit report or even be considered when computing your score.

Vickie Pierre, a college educated adult began her career as a writer. With her first professional job she went to get a car loan. She was turned down because she had poor credit stemming from one missed payment. Because she absolutely needed a car, she had to recruit her brother to co-sign the loan for her. She was hugely embarrassed and vowed it would never happen again. Vickie put a plan together and adjusted her budget and began paying off her debts. In a few years, she was able to raise her credit score from the 600 range to the 800+ range. Vickie pays close attention to her finances now and has vowed to never be in that position again.[3]

Cheat Codes:

Credit is good, necessary, and worth the time and effort to create it. Good credit costs less; Lower interest rates depend entirely upon your credit score and are not available to those with poor credit. Your credit score or FICO score is roughly based on your payment history (35%), how much you owe (30%), age of your credit history (15%), the number of recent credit inquiries (10%) and the type of credit you have (long term or short term). A bad credit score can be repaired with time and directed effort.

Up Next:

Do you know how to evaluate the pros and cons of a loan? Most adults do not know how to do this correctly. If you learn this skill, you will be able to save thousands of dollars and avoid unscrupulous lenders taking advantage of you. Keep reading to learn an easy method of making these comparisons.

Online Game:

Learn about credit and credit scores with this game:
https://www.creditclash.com

13

An Essential Money Game Skill: Comparing Loans

"Remember that credit is money." — **Benjamin Franklin**

One of the founding fathers of our country, scientist, investor, writer, and printer was Benjamin Franklin. His life was not only an amazing adventure, but he was a virtual money genius! For example, in 1789 Franklin gave the City of Boston and the City of Philadelphia the equivalent of $4,400. The money was to be placed in a compound-interest earning account. After 100 years, the cities could access part of the money. After 200 years, the cities could access all the money. The money was only to be used to loan to young tradespeople starting out in business. After 200 years, the money has grown to a whopping $6.5 million. This benefit to citizens in these cities is an awesome tribute to the power of compounding interest and Franklin's knowledge of finances.[1]

Can you tell which loan is better?
- Car Loan #1: $27,250 loan for 3 years at 4.5% interest
- Car Loan #2: $27,250 loan for 7 years at 4.5% interest.

We will come back to this question later in the chapter.

In the money game, you need to level up and gain an important skill that will help you prosper in the future. During your life, circumstances will occur that require a loan. Some loans are pretty good deals and others are terrible. Comparing loans, therefore, is an essential Money Game skill that you need to cultivate.

Choosing a loan from a dozen different options can be very confusing. How could you possibly know which loan is best? With just a little knowledge you can cut through the fog surrounding loans and see them clearly in order to make an informed choice. Let's start with a few basic loan terms so you are on the same page:

Loan: A sum of money that you borrow. Typically, you pay back the borrowed money, plus interest on that money and any fees the lender charges.

Every loan is composed of four variable components:
1. **Principle:** the amount borrowed.
2. **Interest Rate:** the fee you pay on your loan for borrowing the lender's money
3. **Term:** length of loan
4. **Fees charged to write and administer the loan.** Here are some common fees you can expect to pay when you borrow money:
   a. **Application Fee:** A fee charged to a potential borrower for processing (underwriting) most loan applications.
   b. **Origination Fee:** An upfront fee charged for a new loan application, usually quoted as a percentage of the total loan and ranges somewhere between 0.5% and 8% or more of the loan's total.

   c. **Prepayment Fee:** A fee for paying off the loan early to assure the lenders make a certain level of profit. Ask before you close (formally sign the paperwork and are legally bound by the terms of the contract) if a pre-payment fee or penalty exists and how much it is.

   d. **Late Payment Fee:** A substantial fee for paying the monthly payment past its due date. The fee can be either a set amount or a percentage of the payment.

THE 4 ELEMENTS OF A LOAN:

Earlier in the book, I stated that people who get rich avoid consumer debt like the plague. The rich rarely borrow money for consumer items like cars or houses. The rich do frequently, however, borrow money to start new businesses to create wealth.

Billionaire Richard Branson tried to write for his high school's monthly magazine, but his articles were rejected because he was considered far too radical for the very traditional high school publication. As an alternative, Branson applied for a business startup loan and founded a new business that published Student Magazine, *an independent monthly magazine for high school students. Soon after starting his magazine, he borrowed about $2,000 (in today's money) from his mom to pay some bills that had stacked up on his new business.[2] From that point on,* Student Magazine *did extremely well because it focused on subjects that high school students were interested in, such as music and the Vietnam War.*

Branson's high school principal, who we assume heard of the magazine's success, soon gave Branson the ultimatum to either quit the magazine or leave school. Branson left high school and never looked back.[3] His parents were both entrepreneurs as well and were supportive of his choice since it was pretty obvious the traditional school environment was not working for Branson anyway. Of course, Richard Branson went on to become one of the richest men in the world.

The most popular sources of business loans are parents, relatives and friends who believe in your idea and lend you money. The next most popular source is a formal loan from a lender. Branson recommends bypassing traditional banks and connecting with online lenders to fund your new business. Investopedia recommends trying the following online sites for a business loan:[4]

kabbage.com
fundbox.com
fundera.com
kiva.com

Business loans can be risky. You are obligated to pay back all loans and interest. While a loan is your liability, a loan is a lender's financial investment. Either a person, a corporation or perhaps a bank is making money from you via interest and fees charged for your loan. In fact, making money by charging you interest (the fee or profit for the loan) is the reason they are willing to loan you their money in the first place. They are buying an asset (interest-paying investment product), while you are purchasing a liability (what all loans are) until it is paid off.

If you take out a personal loan to start a business—typically the only type of loan a startup business can obtain—you are on the hook personally for that loan. If your new business goes belly-up, you still have the responsibility of repaying that loan. If you borrow money from friends or relatives, understand that you are personally on the hook for repaying that loan as well—unless it is specified (in writing) the loan was to the business and not yours personally.

Let's begin building your loan analysis skillset by helping your friend Douglas purchase a new car. Douglas is twenty-one years old and has had a decent job at a tech contracting company for a couple years now. His old car is run down and has close to 150,000 miles on it. It needs a lot of repairs to keep it running. Douglas has decided the time has come to buy a modestly priced new car. This will be the first new car he has ever purchased. As Douglas begins shopping around, he finds a basic Subaru Forester that he likes. His next step is locating a loan that is within his budget.

Douglas does not know a lot about loans, but he does understand that a higher interest rate means he will have to make a higher monthly payment. He also knows that a higher interest rate means that he will pay more for the car. Douglas, therefore, is looking for a loan with a low interest rate.

Since you know your friend Douglas is looking for a car, you also mention to him that the term period (length of the loan) is just as critical as the interest rate. Although a longer time period will lessen Douglas' monthly payments, it will absolutely increase his overall costs.

To illustrate this point, you show your friend Douglas an online car loan calculator at https://www.calculator.net/auto-loan-calculator.html where he can determine the costs of the various loans he is considering.

The loan he enters assumes a down payment of $10,000 on a vehicle that costs $30,000. Real loans are a little more complicated than this stripped-down example, which does not include the various fees and a variety of state and local taxes.

- Car Loan #1: $20,000 loan for 3 years at 4.5% interest
- Car Loan #2: $20,000 loan for 7 years at 4.5% interest.

Evaluating the two loans:

1. In the first loan, his payment will be a whopping $595.00 a month; however, the payment is only for 3 years.
2. In the second car loan, his monthly payment is a mere $278 a month, but the payment is for 7 long years.

From these two potential loans, most people would likely choose car loan #2 because the monthly payment is so much more affordable and budget friendly, even though loan #2 is for a much longer period of time. On the surface, this seems like a no-brainer, until you look at the total costs.

1. In the first loan, Douglas will pay a modest $1,418 in interest and pay a grand total of $31,418.
2. In the second loan, Douglas will pay $3,352 in interest charges, for a grand total of $33,352.

Now Douglas can make an informed choice about which loan meets his needs.

Using the first loan calculator listed above, you are able to create this simple chart to help Douglas make up his mind:

Down Payment	Loan Total	Interest Rate (APR)	Loan Length	Monthly Payment	Total Interest paid	Total Amount Paid
$10,000	$20,000	4.5%	36 Months	$594.94	$1,418	$31,418
$10,000	$20,000	4.5%	84 months	$278.00	$3,352	$33,352

Your chart contains the four variables Douglas needs to consider when choosing a loan:

1. **Principle:** the amount borrowed
2. **Interest Rate:** the fee you pay for borrowing the lender's money
3. **Term:** length of loan
4. **Fees** (see next section)

Douglas notices there is no fee column on the above chart and asks you why. You tell your friend that some lenders might advertise a loan with a low interest rate to get him in the door. When he obtains the loan paperwork, however, he could suddenly find he is signing papers that quote a much higher interest rate. Comparing loans is difficult when hidden fees are thrown into your deal. Luckily, you tell him a super easy way to compare the costs of various loan fees thanks to our government passing a law called the Truth in Lending Act (1968). This law requires fees to be rolled into the interest rate and disclosed to you as the annual total cost of the loan being proposed, which is known as the Annual Percentage Rate (APR). All lenders must provide you with the APR for their loans.

> Always look for the APR (the interest rate plus all the fees rolled into one rate) when considering a loan, which is likely higher than the loan's advertised interest rate.

An increase in the interest rate or one of the other variables in the equation radically changes the overall results. One final note, how often an interest rate compounds (an interest charge on both the principle and the unpaid interest to date/see glossary of terms) can also impact how much Douglas will pay. Interest rates on loans can compound at any of the following rates:

- Daily
- Monthly
- Quarterly
- Annually

Of the above range of options, daily compounding loans cost slightly more than a monthly compounding loan—and so on. Annually compounding loans cost the least of all the options on this list. Here is a list of common loan types and how often they compound:

- Student Loans = Compound Daily
- Credit Cards = Compound Daily
- Mortgages = Compounded monthly or semi-annually depending on if it is a fixed rate mortgage.
- Car Loans = Usually a simple interest loan- no compounding. More interest is charged at the beginning of the loan.

Douglas decides that he really doesn't like either option. In loan #1, the monthly payment seems way too high for his projected budget. In loan #2, he just doesn't want to pay that long for a car and the total cost is way too much. Douglas instead decides to wait until a few months so he could put more money down on the car to lower his monthly payment. Below is the loan he eventually signed:

Down Payment	Loan Total	Interest Rate (APR)	Loan Length	Monthly Payment	Total Interest Paid	Total Amount Paid
$15,000	$15,000	4.5%	36 Months	$446.20	$1,063	$16,063

As you can see, evaluating loans is a very important financial skill young people need to acquire quickly to win the Money Game. If not, Money Gamers will find themselves victims of loan industry charlatans who are waiting, ready and willing to take advantage of them. It almost seems the poorer you happen to be, the more that people line up to take advantage of you with terrible loan deals. They assume those with poor finances know nothing about loans. Additionally, those with low credit scores or those who have a low income have very limited choices. Here are loan types that are typically designed to take advantage of those who are less fortunate in our society:

Driving down the road you may have seen signs for these types of loans:

Buy Here, Pay Here Loans: A type of loan from used-car dealers. The financing is designed to maximize the dealer's profit from those with poor credit scores who buy their vehicles. They take advantage of low credit score buyers by pricing their cars higher and by charging a very high interest rate. A very aggressive repossession policy is written into the contract so the dealer can take the car back if the buyer falls behind on payments. The same car is then resold to another buyer and the process starts over again with another customer.

Payday Loans: A cash - advance loan offered to those who have a limited ability to obtain credit due to a poor credit score, or to those who don't know they can easily get better deals. These loans have an interest rate of 28% or more, which would be illegal in other situations. The lenders also typically have a very aggressive collections policy. You typically give the lender a post-dated check or access to your checking account to repay the loan and all fees when your next paycheck is due.

Auto Title Loans: If you own a car free and clear (you have a car title), you can use the title as collateral (something you agree to forfeit to the lender if you don't pay your loan) for the loan. In the case of auto title loans, the borrower is charged huge fees on top of extremely high interest rates—such as 300% APR. If the buyer falls behind on payments, the lender takes the car to satisfy the loan.

BATTLE THE LOAN SHARK
IN THE MONEY GAME

CHOOSE YOUR WEAPONS TO BATTLE THE SHARKS!

LOAN CALCULATOR TO SEE ACTUAL RESULTS

A GOOD CREDIT SCORE FOR BEST DEALS

CHART YOUR LOAN

KNOW YOUR LOAN'S APR OR ANNUAL PERCENT RATE

LOW DEBT TO INCOME RATIO FOR BEST DEALS

Cheat Codes:

The four elements of a loan consist of the amount borrowed or the loan's principle, the interest rate (APR), the term or the length of loan and the fees charged by a lender to create the loan. Small changes in any of these elements can create large differences in payment totals. A general principle is the longer a loan's repayment term, the lower the monthly payment will be; However, a longer loan term creates a much larger overall expense—sometimes double the shorter loan's payment total.

The best way to compare loans is to create a simple chart so you can easily see the differences. Use an online calculator to determine the monthly payment, total amount paid and other details of a loan. Dozens of online calculators are designed for many types of loans.

Those with poor credit or few financial resources are targeted by predatory lenders who know the less fortunate have few options and little financial knowledge. If at all possible, avoid payday loans, car title loans, and buy here/pay here loans due to super high interest rates and fees.

Up Next:
In Chapter 3, we discussed the most common financial life regret in America—many people failed to save their money. Creating an emergency fund is a large part of the solution to this regret. Keep reading to see how to accomplish this goal.

Online Game:
Become a shady loan shark and see if you can get rich in this game: https://shadysam.com

14

Savings Powers-up Your Money Game Strength

"Do not save what is left after spending but spend what is
left after saving." — **Warren Buffett**

My wife and I eventually did really well in the savings and
investing department. We were able to put together a net
worth of over a million dollars. Although I am proud of this
accomplishment, I am now left with the certain knowledge that
many of my efforts were misinformed and misdirected. If I had
to do it over again, I could easily be a multi-millionaire. One
of the reasons our efforts were slowed, is that we were partially
blocked by unanticipated barriers that we did not know how to
manage. Luckily for you, I am here to help you manage those
barriers.

The first barrier you must overcome for saving is the normal
psychological desire we all have for instant gratification. We all
crave instant gratification! Instant gratification in the financial world means creating a sense of excitement in the present

by buying things you don't really need. Instant gratification has several sub-categories within it, such as spending money to buy things that are popular, buying things to relieve stress or buying consumer items to impress others.

One of the problems with combatting instant gratification is that you can engage in it without consciously understanding your motivations. For example, if you hang out with friends who all have nice clothes, it is natural for you to pay attention to your wardrobe. You could easily find yourself buying more expensive clothing. After all, you spent time with your friends talking about clothing and looking at clothing, so this becomes something you notice. You almost become desensitized to the extra costs you will pay.

One way to combat this problem is to focus on your goals. If you spend money that is not in your budget or is unrelated to your goals, you will not be able to save money. To those who claim YOLO (you only live once), I say if you can't resist spending frivolously now, you will never be able to afford the next-level items/experiences you truly want. Today, if I (or we) really want to buy something next level, I can afford it and can even pay cash for it if I want. This does not mean that I buy everything I want—no one can, no matter how much money one has. I still consider everything that I purchase carefully in connection with my overall goals and budget.

For example, my wife and I just rented a large, first-class beachfront home for a week and invited the entire family to visit us. We were able to do this without much thought or concern about the cost. We lived for a week at the beach and reconnected with family. This is how waiting to obtain the things you really want and instead focusing on your goals can allow you to prosper in the future.

Another common barrier to saving is putting it off until later. A perfect example of this is the concept of saving for retirement. The saving for retirement marketing push by the financial industry is one of the worst things to happen to Americans. This almost automatic programming has led to millions of Americans associating savings solely with retirement.

Procrastination is natural and puts the task of saving for retirement off until later—usually much later. After all, you're just getting started! The behavior of putting off saving for retirement is called hyperbolic discounting (see glossary), which means that most people put more value on a benefit today rather than what will happen in the future.[1] Over half of Americans self-reported they are way behind in saving for retirement; 16% of this group claim they have no retirement savings at all.[2] A lack of education about the requirement of time for the compounding interest process needed to grow wealth (by saving and investing) contributes to the hyperbolic discounting mistake.[3] This natural tendency to put off saving for retirement is the reason why young people don't save for retirement until they are in their mid-thirties or even in their forties. Only 39% of young people will bother to save for retirement in their twenties.[4] Also, people who have college debt were found to have only half the financial resources of those who had no college debt.[5]

For these reasons and others, I urge you not to think much about saving for retirement. That is entirely the wrong approach. Instead, work on increasing your savings and your net worth today for a better life today. Luckily, a high net worth will also build a great tomorrow. In no way does this mean you should snub retirement accounts that are perfectly designed to help in wealth-building efforts.

3 BARRIERS TO SAVING

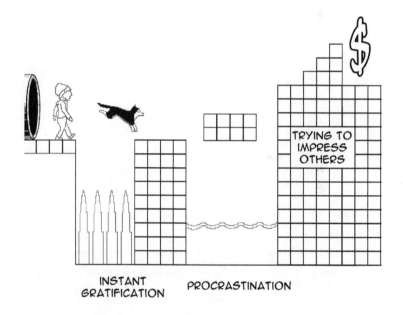

My wife knows sisters Maria and Tina very well. Maria, the younger sister, saved and invested $2,000 annually from age 19-26 (just eight years). After age 26, she stopped investing additional money. She earned a compounded interest rate of approximately 7% annually. When she turned 65 years of age, she had over $300,000 in her investment account. Her total investment, however, was only $16,000.

    Tina, the older sister, did not want Maria to get ahead of her in the investing department. However, since she waited until later in life (age 30) to begin saving and investing, she needed to invest $2,000 for 31 years to catch up to Maria. Her total investment turned out to be a whopping $64,000 (at 7% compounded interest annually) to make around the same amount as her younger sister Maria. Because Tina waited to save and invest, it cost her an additional $48,000 to generate approximately the same $300,000 as her sister because she missed out on the very precious first eight years of compounding interest. Check out the chart below for details:

Age	Maria		Tina	
19	$ 2,000	$ 2,140		
20	$ 2,000	$ 4,430		
21	$ 2,000	$ 6,880		
22	$ 2,000	$ 9,501		
23	$ 2,000	$ 12,307		
24	$ 2,000	$ 15,308		
25	$ 2,000	$ 18,520		
26	$ 2,000	$ 21,956		
27		$ 23,493		
28		$ 25,137		
29		$ 26,897		
30		$ 28,780	$ 2,000	$ 2,140
31		$ 30,794	$ 2,000	$ 4,430
32		$ 32,950	$ 2,000	$ 6,880
33		$ 35,257	$ 2,000	$ 9,501
34		$ 37,724	$ 2,000	$ 12,307
35		$ 40,365	$ 2,000	$ 15,308
36		$ 43,191	$ 2,000	$ 18,520
37		$ 46,214	$ 2,000	$ 21,956

38		$ 49,449	$ 2,000	$ 25,633
39		$ 52,911	$ 2,000	$ 29,567
40		$ 56,614	$ 2,000	$ 33,777
41		$ 60,577	$ 2,000	$ 38,281
42		$ 64,818	$ 2,000	$ 43,101
43		$ 69,355	$ 2,000	$ 48,258
44		$ 74,210	$ 2,000	$ 53,776
45		$ 79,404	$ 2,000	$ 59,680
46		$ 84,963	$ 2,000	$ 65,998
47		$ 90,910	$ 2,000	$ 72,758
48		$ 97,274	$ 2,000	$ 79,991
49		$ 104,083	$ 2,000	$ 87,730
50		$ 111,369	$ 2,000	$ 96,011
51		$ 119,165	$ 2,000	$ 104,872
52		$ 127,506	$ 2,000	$ 114,353
53		$ 136,432	$ 2,000	$ 124,498
54		$ 145,982	$ 2,000	$ 135,353
55		$ 156,200	$ 2,000	$ 146,968
56		$ 167,135	$ 2,000	$ 159,395
57		$ 178,834	$ 2,000	$ 172,693
58		$ 191,352	$ 2,000	$ 186,922
59		$ 204,747	$ 2,000	$ 202,146
60		$ 219,079	$ 2,000	$ 218,436
61		$ 234,415	$ 2,000	$ 235,867
62		$ 250,824		$ 252,378
63		$ 268,381		$ 270,044
64		$ 287,168		$ 288,947
Age 65		$ 307,270		$ 309,173
Total Contributions:	$ 16,000		$ 64,000	
Years of Contributions:	8		32	

SISTERS

**YOUNGER
SISTER
MARIA**
SAVED &
INVESTED
$2000/ YEAR
FROM AGE
19-26.
REQUIRED
$16,000

**OLDER
SISTER
TINA**
SAVED &
INVESTED
$2000/ YEAR
FROM AGE
30-61.
REQUIRED
$64,000

AT AGE 65 BOTH NOW HAVE APPROX $300,000

WAITING 8 YEARS COST
TINA $48,000 MORE
TO REACH THE SAME
$300,000

WHICH SISTER WOULD YOU RATHER BE?

START SAVING & INVESTING
ASAP!

*ASSUME 7%
ANNUAL RETURN
ON INVESTMENTS

Retirement is just one of the many terrific benefits of having a high net worth. In the present, savings will provide you with more freedom, less stress, less anxiety, greater self-esteem, greater pride, and greater domestic harmony.[6] Having a high net worth will give you the confidence to try to conquer new frontiers and take on exciting new goals.

Using your financial resources in an attempt to impress others is another barrier to saving. A great example of this is when you want to attract a romantic partner. Trying to woo someone with a flashy car or a nice residence is a losing game. In reality, if you are single, saving and building up your financial resources will make you more attractive to a potential life partner! If it doesn't, you should probably rethink your choice.

In a study published by *Frontiers in Psychology* (2020), having "adequate resources" is a basic requirement for both men and women. The results of this study refer not only to money, but also adequate time to commit to a relationship. Also, women who took the time and effort to develop their own financial resources pay even more attention to potential mates' financial abilities, how they spend their time and their moral character. Men who developed their own financial resources also pay more attention to a potential mate's financial ability.[7]

Like many, I was caught up in society's rat race even though I knew better. I was concerned about having a nice home, having a really nice car, and living in a nice neighborhood. Why was I caught up in societal perceptions, even when I knew better? After years of reflection, I now understand that one of the reasons I was so concerned about perceptions is that I was looking for a significant other. That was a serious misstep. I mistakenly thought societal signs of affluence would help with that quest. For the record, this was the wrong approach and I paid the price for it through two unhappy marriages and eventual divorces. In the next marriage, I made it a priority to find someone who shared my goals of creating financial independence and a life of freedom.

Some people just don't have the background or perspective needed to value financial independence because they don't even really understand the concept or the benefits of an abundant financial life. If you can teach them, and they are on board, that is great. It is just essential that you pick a romantic partner who makes financial independence a life priority. If you get into a committed relationship without this shared goal, financial independence is much less likely to happen. It is much easier to make sure everyone is on the same page in the beginning of a relationship (with the same values and life goals) than it is to expect someone to change later.

"I don't want broke men; you need to be financially sound before you can date me." — Juliet Ibrahim

Actress, YouTuber, and influencer Juliet Ibrahim revealed that she still has hope of marrying again after her divorce from the CEO of Kantanka motors, Sarfo Kantanka. She made it clear, however, that to date her, you must have your finances in order. She will not even consider settling down with a broke man, even if he is family oriented. She wants someone whose energy will match her own. She wants an equal partner, not someone she will have to take care of.[8]

If some magic should happen and I had this all to do over again, I would have begun my financial journey entirely differently. Back when I was young, I would have lived as cheaply as possible and saved and then invested every dime I could earn. The benefit of doing so increases exponentially as time passes. I would have also learned more about investing right away, rather than waiting until later to learn this valuable information. By far, these were my two biggest mistakes. I pass them on to you so that you can learn from them. Also, I want you to know that building wealth is absolutely worth the effort. My wife and I have almost zero financial stress and more freedom than anyone else we know. Neither of us would change places with almost anyone.

Cheat Codes:

Instant gratification is a savings barrier for everyone. Sometimes you can engage in instant gratification and not even realize it until later. The way to avoid the pull of instant gratification is to stay focused on achieving your goals. Don't fall prey to the trap of saving for retirement. This mindset allows you to put off saving until later. The tendency we have to put off doing positive things for our future is called hyperbolic discounting. Forget retirement and save now to build wealth now. That in no way means we should snub retirement accounts in our wealth-building efforts. Additionally, trying to attract a potential romantic partner with the cosmetic trappings of being a successful person is a loser. Instead, find someone that values financial abundance and stability.

Up Next:

After you create adequate savings, move to the next level of the Money Game, which is investing. Investing grows your money into a proper fortune—the very pinnacle of master level Money Game play.

Online Game:

Online banking and budget simulator game:
http://obanksimulator.ngpf.org/index.php

15

Investing Is Master Level Play

"Work smarter, not harder." — Allen F. Morgenstern

llen Morgenstern was an industrial engineer who helped pioneer work improvement systems. His goal was to improve a work process so a manufacturer could produce more goods with less effort, thereby increasing production output. Although Morgenstern didn't talk about investing as part of his "work smarter not harder" paradigm, he should have. Let's put it this way, do you want to work your whole life until your health prevents you from working any longer and then live with meager means until you pass away? I would rather invest a percentage of my wages every paycheck so that later, I need not work at all because my investments produce enough money to replace my wages. Most people, I believe, would choose this second path as well.

Congratulations on getting to Level 5, which is master level Money Game play. To begin your coaching on this level, let's talk about mindsets. Most working people, to make their lives easier and less stressful, typically spend their money on consumer items that distract them from their everyday work and life stressors. This spending, if not closely monitored and controlled, leaves them with few financial resources in the present and significant debts to pay in the future.

> The standard behavior in America is to get trapped in a cycle of working hard and then spending to relieve stress, which leaves half of all Americans with virtually no financial resources.

The goal is to engage in behaviors that are the exact opposite of this common life path. Investing can lead to a better life that does not involve working for your daily, weekly or monthly income. This may sound like a giant scam to lots of people. Yet, thousands and thousands of people have done it in the past and thousands more will do it again in the future.

My wife and I now make more income annually from our investments than we received in wages from our jobs when we worked, which means we no longer require jobs at all unless we just wish to work. The cross-over point is when working people eventually make more income from their investments than they made in annual wages from their jobs.

> The strategy thousands of people have success-fully used to build prosperity is a focused effort of converting their weekly working wages into assets (investments that create a profit) that will generate income and/or grow in value over time.

YOU INVEST BY BUYING ASSETS

YOU BUY
ASSETS THAT:

1. MAKE A PROFIT
   AND/OR

2. "APPRECIATE"
   OVER TIME

Once assets are purchased, they can earn income, which can then be reinvested or the investments you bought may increase in value over time—or both situations could even occur simultaneously.

For example, if you bought an apartment building and you made a profit each month, you could use your monthly profit to purchase even more apartment buildings (investments), which is called reinvesting. If your apartment building also increased in value over time, you have created a profit for your use later when you sell all or part of this investment.

I am now going to discuss a variety of investments for the remainder of the book. So that everyone is on the same page, below are definitions of the most common investments.

- **Stocks:** The ownership of a small portion (or a share) of a corporation that entitles the owner to a share in the profits and assets of the corporation, equal to their ownership of the number of stocks they possess. For example, if they own 100 out of a corporation's 1,000 stocks, they own 10% of that corporation. Stock purchases range from risky (the corporation may go broke) to secure (an extremely large and stable corporation in the U.S. that is doing well). If you have a stock and decide you no longer want it, you can sell the stock for its going rate on the stock exchange (where stocks are bought and sold).

- **Bonds:** Bonds are a loan investment product (essentially a loan contract) you buy. The bond is an IOU, or a loan, issued by entities that need an inflow of cash. Bonds can be issued by the federal, state, or local government or other specific government entities like a transit authority or even by foreign governments. Other classes of bonds can be issued by businesses such as corporations. Bonds can be resold by you to other investors if you chose to do so.

  ° Coupon Rate: the amount of interest the bond will pay you over the life of the loan period

- ° Par: face value on the bond
- ° Call Date: a bond's maturity date (when the bond ends)
- **Cash**: Money is sometimes held in reserve in your investing account and is also considered its own category. Cash increases or decreases in value depending on economic conditions.

Investments are the exact opposite of a loan or debt you must pay. Instead of paying out money on a loan, each month you collect a profit that increases your prosperity. The big picture is that you buy investments and then you reinvest your profits to increase your wealth even more over time, which creates the impact of compounding interest. For example, if I made $10 from the $100 I have invested in a stock fund, then I made a profit of 10% that year. If I reinvest my $10 profit back into that investment, that gives me $110. If I make the same 10% the following year, I will now receive $11 profit (10% of the $110 earns me $121), which is how you create compound interest from investing. Although an extra dollar here or there does not sound like a lot of money, investments and their profits can snowball to eventually generate thousands and thousands of dollars.

Another way to supercharge your investments is through the purchase of stocks. Stocks are a piece of corporate ownership. Sometimes corporations distribute their annual profits to their owners. If the owner then reinvests their corporate profits by buying more stocks, it may create even more profit for them.

The first million dollars my wife and I created was by investing (or buying assets) with money from our paychecks that we routed into our employers' retirement accounts (a 401K). We started small and built up the amount we routed to our investment accounts. We primarily bought stocks, bonds, and real estate in these accounts. By the time we finished, a little over 20 years later, half of our pay was going towards purchasing new investments. Over the years, the money we invested from our paychecks only totaled around $333,333. Yet, we grew that amount to just over $1 million in under 25 years through the power of reinvesting that created the impact of compounding interest.

Since that time, we have used some of that money for world traveling, but most of it stays put and has continued to grow. We recently crushed the $1.5 million dollar mark and are still growing strong. How much money did we contribute to climb over the $1.5 million mark? The answer is almost zero! That's right, all we did was get out of the way and let our investments continue to grow while using our other income streams (which I listed in chapter 7) to live. In just a few years, we expect to hit the $2 million mark, even though we plan to contribute next to nothing to the money pile and may even use more of it.

Let me give you a hypothetical example that illustrates the point for young graduates:

Kaley is a young adult who is working full-time and attends college part time. One day her parents told her, "Kaley, we want you to know that your grandma passed away and she left you $75,000 in her will." Kaley is a money-smart young lady and does not want to waste this golden opportunity her grandmother created for her. She goes to investor.gov and uses the website's compound interest calculator.[1] She enters the amount her grandmother has left her and finds that if she makes anywhere from 9% to 15% return on her investments over the next twenty years (very doable over a long period of time), she will *have over $1 million. Not only that, upward of several million might be possible, depending upon luck and the investments she chooses.*

Because she is really smart, Kaley also completed a financial investing plan that lays out her plan and investment portfolio (a mix of stocks, bonds, and cash) she plans to use to succeed with her investing. Her parents are thrilled with her plan.

Kaley's Simple Investment Plan:

Simple Investment Plan	
Review Current Finances	I continue to live my current lifestyle and work in my current job while attending college part time.
Lump Sum Added	Invest my $75,000 in a Fidelity investment account (see chapter 16 and the heading "How to Get Started" to learn how to open a Fidelity account.
Amount: How much I need to add monthly into my investment account?	Each paycheck I will invest $50.00 into my investment account. I will increase the amount I invest every year.

Simple Investment Plan	
Risk Tolerance: How much risk can I stand? (Risk of losing money instead of making money) A riskier investment, however, may generally create a higher profit.	Risk tolerance is very high given the long timeline. Generally, stocks are riskier than bonds, but can create a higher profit when they are winners. You can typically tolerate a riskier portfolio mix (portfolio with more stocks than bonds and cash), the younger you are because you have a long time for stocks to rise overall. (This will be explained in the next chapter.)
Choose an Investment Strategy. What type of investments will you purchase?	Create a portfolio mix of stocks, bonds, and cash based on your risk tolerance. My initial mix will be approximately 80% stocks, 15% in bonds and 5% in cash. (More information in the following chapters)
Monitor As Needed	Check investments at least annually to determine if the investment portfolio needs rebalancing (buying and selling to get back to the original percentages). Many times, due to profits rising or falling, the investment mix gets out of balance. The strategy is to sell some and buy other investment types in order to move it back to your original percentages.
Tax Planning	Consult with a tax planning professional (my parents' tax person) to minimize tax liability.

The extremely important lesson you should absorb from this story is the awesome power of compounding interest. The next important lesson is that Kaley did not simply throw money at investments in a haphazard manner. She used investing principles such as reinvesting her profits and selecting a mix of investments to create wealth. In short, she created an investing plan that outlined a well-proven, simple investing strategy.

IF YOU ARE GIFTED A LARGE SUM OF MONEY, IS COLLEGE THE BEST USE FOR YOUR FUNDS?

IN *SOME* CASES, LONG TERM INVESTING COULD BE A BETTER CHOICE, ESPECIALLY IF YOU DON'T FEEL A STRONG CALLING FOR A PARTICULAR DEGREE.

Cheat Codes:

Average people like you and I can harness the power of compounding interest for our benefit. We do this by buying investments (investing) and by reinvesting our profits from those investments. More investments create even more profit and so on. Reinvesting mimics compounding interest, such as you would pay out to a credit card company. The only difference is now you receive compounding interest instead of paying it. The goal is to replace a job's income with investment income freeing us from being required to work at a job in the future—called the crossover point. The most common investments people buy for their portfolio include stocks and bonds that are readily available in your employer's retirement accounts.

Up Next:

If you are going to invest, it is essential you learn how investing works and how to succeed in creating the forward financial momentum you need to create prosperity. The next chapter explains stocks and how the stock market works.

Online Game:

https://www.howthemarketworks.com

16

Master Game Level Play: How the Stock Market Works

"Truly wealthy people develop the habit of 'getting rich slow' rather than 'getting rich quick.'" — **Brian Tracy**

Brain Tracy was from a very poor family in Vancouver, Canada. He was a kid that always seemed to be in trouble. His family was so poor that he and his brothers always wore clothes given to them from organizations, people or families that helped those in need.

Tracy dropped out of school at an early age and spent his time working manual labor jobs. At 20, Brian decided to travel the world and began by catching a ship to England. He traveled across Europe and had many adventures and close calls with serious injury or death. One morning, Brian woke up and decided he wanted to change his life. He realized that his life was entirely his responsibility. From this thought process, he developed a "no excuse philosophy." His no excuse philosophy also encompassed a life view that it is your responsibility to view your life in a positive manner and create the best attitude possible. A good attitude is absolutely essential to creating favorable outcomes—otherwise you will not have the energy and drive needed to succeed.

Tracy began a career in sales and was hugely successful. He then moved into real estate, marketing and then investing. Later, Tracy began motivational and life training to help others succeed in life. One of Tracy's philosophies is that you become what you think about! He noted that the rich think a lot about "financial independence" and that is what they achieve.[1] Tracy is a great writer and I have read several of his books about creating success and accomplishing goals.

The time has now come for you to learn how investing in the stock market works, essential knowledge for a master player who is on a quest to conquer their Money Game. Most people have no clue about how the stock market works. They don't really understand what a stock is, how to buy them, or how owning a stock can increase their wealth over time. This is a significant failing of our educational system. Luckily, I am here to help you fill in this gap with this stock market primer.

How The Stock Market Works

As mentioned in the previous chapter, when you buy a corporation's stock you are buying a small portion (or share) of that corporation. We buy corporations (various stocks) so that we can make a profit in the future. This process is called investing, which is a business term that means you buy an asset (in this case, a company's stock) to make a profit later. If you buy something where there is no expectation of a future profit, the purchase is neither investing nor an investment.

Many times, the word "company" is used generically in investing discussions to mean a corporation, although the term is not completely accurate as you will learn. A corporation must have a very specific legal structure and companies are not required to have a specific structure.

Owning a stock not only gives you a "share" in the profits and partial ownership of the assets of your newly purchased company, but it also allows you to vote for the board of directors. The board provides overall managerial direction to the corporation—a legal requirement for all corporations. The board of directors hires and fires the corporation's senior managers or the corporation's officers. The board has a fiduciary requirement, meaning they must always act in the shareholders' financial best interests. The board members typically must be shareholders, although some stock exchanges (such as New York Stock Exchange) require some independent board members. The officers follow the board's overall direction and strategy. If the officers fail to perform, they are replaced by the board.

Stock Exchanges:

Stocks are bought and sold on a stock exchange. The broader term for a stock exchange is the stock market. Individual investors or corporations are free to buy and sell stocks on designated controlled stock exchanges located in nearly every country in the world. Examples of exchanges include the New York Stock Exchange, the London Stock Exchange and the Shanghai Stock Exchange. A variety of different investments (often called securities) such as stocks and bonds can be bought and sold on these exchanges. All stock exchanges are electronically connected through the secure Electronic Communications Network (ECN).

Primary Stock Exchanges in the USA:

1. New York Stock Exchange
2. Chicago Board Options Exchange
3. NYSE Chicago (New York Stock Exchange in Chicago)
4. Boston Stock Exchange

5. NASDAQ (National Association of Securities Dealers Automatic Quotation System, NY)
6. Philadelphia Stock Exchange
7. NYSE Arca (New York Stock Exchange and Archipelago)
8. American Stock Exchange (in New York)
9. IEX (Investors Stock Exchange in New York)
10. Miami Stock Exchange

Why Stock Prices Fluctuate:
Stock prices are based upon investors' evaluations of the supply and demand for the company, publicly available financial information about the company, and a myriad of other things. Here is just a partial list of issues that impact stock prices:

- The general economy's direction
- Profits made by the company in the past
- The company's profitability compared to similar companies in that business sector
- News about the company
- Direction of the world's economy
- Investor psychology (an entire field of study)
- Changing technology that impacts the company
- Corruption scandals coming to light in the company
- Changes in government policy and laws that impact the company

All of these factors coming together is why it is impossible to predict future prices in the stock market in the short-term. Long-term prices have historically gone up.

STOCK PRICES

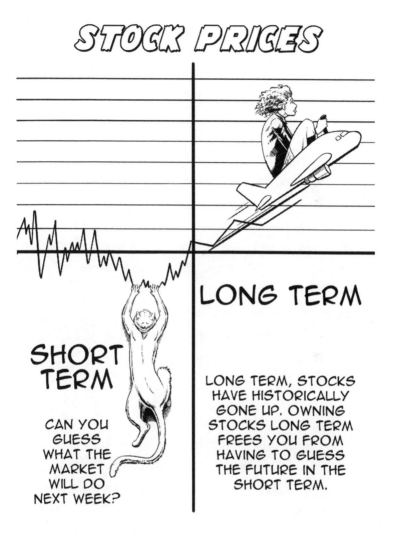

LONG TERM

SHORT TERM

CAN YOU GUESS WHAT THE MARKET WILL DO NEXT WEEK?

LONG TERM, STOCKS HAVE HISTORICALLY GONE UP. OWNING STOCKS LONG TERM FREES YOU FROM HAVING TO GUESS THE FUTURE IN THE SHORT TERM.

Where Stocks Originate:

Stocks are initially created by the corporation's owners (usually the founders or first investors who began the company) who decide they need to raise more money to fund their company's expansion efforts typically because they have many more orders than products to fill those orders. To fund such an expansion, the corporation decides to sell partial ownership of itself to the public through an Initial Public Offering (IPO) on a stock exchange. Their hope is that even though they are selling partial ownership, the expansion will make the corporation much more valuable for everyone involved.

The amount of shares initially issued is determined by the owners and an investment bank at the time the shares are issued. An investment bank buys all of the new stocks and gives the corporation some money up front to get started with their expansion—called underwriting. The money will be used to purchase a building, machines, hire employees or whatever is needed to expand the business' operations to make it larger and more profitable. The bank then sells the stock on a stock exchange to make back their money and maybe even create a profit.

Public And Private Corporations:

Now is a good time to explain more about the legal structure of private corporations and public corporations. The term corporation in this context means the company has become its own "legal person" and has the right to take out loans and enter into contracts entirely independent of its owners. The significance of this legal designation is that it protects the owners from liability stemming from the corporation's actions. For example, if a corporation were to go broke or even be sued out of existence in civil court, the owners are not personally liable for loss, debts or civil damages. Therefore, if you own all or part of a corporation that goes broke, you will only lose the money you spent to buy the stocks. No one can come after you for the corporation's unpaid bills or an unpaid lawsuit.

WHERE STOCKS COME FROM

DAD STOCKS ♡ MOM STOCKS

BABY STOCKS

OUR TEAM CREATES A SUNGLASSES MANUFACTURING CO.

COMPANY HAS MORE ORDERS THAN PRODUCTS, SO THEY WANT TO EXPAND.

INVENTORY

THEY SELL PART OF COMPANY TO RAISE MONEY TO EXPAND.

BANK GIVES THEM MONEY TO EXPAND AND TAKES STOCK FOR RESALE.

INVESTMENT BANK

BANK SELLS STOCKS ON THE STOCK EXCHANGE & TRIES TO MAKE A PROFIT.

STOCKS =

SUNGLASSES CO. EXPANDS AND MAKES MORE PROFITS FOR ALL OWNERS.

The majority of private corporations are organized under state law—usually to protect the owner(s) from civil liability. Private corporations have fewer controls placed on them from the federal government and conduct their business as the owner(s) feel it should be conducted—within legal reason. To be able to sell shares of stock on the stock exchange, however, a corporation must go public or become a public corporation organized under federal law.

The federal laws regarding corporations are enforced by the Securities and Exchange Commission (SEC). The SEC is the federal agency that assures corporations follow the corporate structure requirements, accounting rules and various other laws. For example, the SEC mandates certain accounting practices be used to assure fairness and transparency, which means corporations must follow best accounting practices that are generally the industry standard. These accounting practices are mandated so that potential investors can rely on a company's quarterly reports to decide to invest or not invest in a particular corporation. Creating a false impression of the company's profitability through accounting practices or misrepresentation is illegal and may result in an investigation and likely arrests by the SEC or other federal agencies.

All public corporations must produce an annual report, which explains the corporation's financial status, market share, the year's past activities and their view of the corporation's future. Current shareholders and potential investors should read these reports thoroughly to determine the company's risk and the potential future rewards for their investment(s).

Types of Stock:

1. **Common stocks** give the owner a voting right in how the corporation is run, maintained and its business strategy.
2. **Preferred stocks** do not allow voting privileges, but the owner receives dividends (cash payments) of the corporation's profits before common stockholders receive a share of the profits. In case the corporation is dissolved,

preferred shareholders are given their cut of the corporation's assets (if there are any) first. In that way, a preferred stock has some similarities to a bond (A bond is a loan you make to the government, a company or special government organization that agrees to pay the money back with interest); however, preferred stocks still represent company ownership.

Risk is Present in Every Stock:

Stocks of companies go up and down in price. An investor, therefore, faces two basic types of risks for losing their money.

1. **Systematic risk** has to do with a downturn in our economy and generally drags nearly all stocks/corporations lower in value—at least temporarily. The stock owner will see the value of companies sink lower.

2. **Non-systematic risk** is when a company or a particular industry does poorly because of changing economic conditions, incorrect strategies or a poorly run corporation. In such a situation, your stock's value could even drop to zero.

You can reduce investor risk by owning a wide variety of stocks and other investments. This strategy has been scientifically proven to somewhat reduce both systematic and non-systematic risk for individual investors.

Fitting It All Together:

Brandon Fleisher of Toronto, Canada learned about stocks in his 8th grade math class. The class exercise involved picking a stock and following it to see how it performed. Brandon picked Avalon

Rare Metals(on paper, not in real life), which soon hit a record high price. Brandon was intrigued and began regularly investing on paper and following his picks' progress over several years. He did so well at this paper exercise, his parents funded a stock market account with $48K when he was sixteen. In one year, Brandon tripled his money by investing in smaller companies he correctly anticipated would grow based on the research he did on these companies. The companies he chose (Tesla being one of them) roughly tripled in value in one year. Brandon is known for doing extensive research on any company he buys. He is even known to call the corporation's Chief Executive Officer (CEO) to ask questions about stock reports. [2]

I am not an individual stock picking person. I do not recommend this strategy to you. Instead, the vast majority of my investments are stock mutual funds (see next paragraph) to reduce investment risk and increase my profits.

Now let's switch gears and talk about a very popular investment called a stock mutual fund, which is a type of "holding company/ investment corporation" that buys and sells shares of stocks (or other investments) in a professionally designed and managed strategy. A professional investment manager is hired by the mutual fund to purchase stocks, bonds, real estate or other investments to pursue the investing strategy the corporation advertised to its customers or shareholders. Investors actually buy stocks or shares of the mutual fund, not the actual stocks. Technically, the mutual fund owns all the individual shares of stock. The mutual fund is, in turn, owned by its individual investors. The mutual fund will automatically reinvest your profits into your mutual account and thereby create the impact of compounding interest.

Stocks are Not a Get-Rich-Quick Method of Investing:

I don't want to leave you with the wrong impression about stock trading (a term for buying and selling stocks). Short term traders who jump in and out of stocks (called day-traders because sometimes they only hold stock for a day or so) almost always lose money in the long run. In fact, most lose so much money they can't sustain their short-term trading strategy for very long. For example, here are several statistics that clarify this issue:

- Only 1% of short-term traders make money once fees (for buying and selling stocks) are taken into consideration.[3]
- 40% of short-term traders quit after one month.
- 80% of short-term traders quit within two years.
- 13% that are left quit after three years.
- 7% that are left quit after five years.[4]

My experience supports what we see in the above statistics. For example, during a stock market boom (stocks were broadly rising in value), a man I know removed all his money from his pension plan that he worked years to create—which of course ended his monthly pension. He used the money for short-term stock trades, thinking he could make more money than his small pension payment. He was influenced to do this by unscrupulous salespeople who convinced him through the marketing of their day-trading course that they could teach him to become a successful and rich day trader. Within a few months he lost all of his money, which is one of the reasons it is very important to understand risk. Also, this is a dire warning about which sources to trust in investing.

At my workplace, we would have contests to determine who could make the most money in the stock market (very similar to a fantasy football league). We would each have a hypothetical amount of money.

We decided (hypothetically) how much each trade would cost. Based on the performance of the stocks we bought and sold on paper, we would see who ended up with the most money. Short-term traders always lost this contest! The winners bought mutual funds of larger companies that paid dividends and then held them for the duration of the contest. They at least made money on dividends, and they had minimal fees to subtract from their profits.

The Best Winning Stock Investment Strategy:

Just like Brian Tracy's quote about not trying to get rich quick, buying and holding stocks is the strategy to win in the stock market game. Prices might fluctuate in the short term, but in the long term, people who buy and hold stocks usually win! Stocks have historically gone up over the long run—just like everything else in life. This buy and hold strategy eliminates the need to figure out which stocks will be short-term winners or the need to decide when the stock prices are at their highest price and likely to go down in price soon. Luckily, the simplest strategy that requires the least amount of effort from you is typically the clear winner.[5]

I want to re-emphasize one final issue with stocks. All investing involves the risk that you could lose some or all of the money you invest. There is never a guarantee you will obtain the intended profits. Some investments have higher risks and some investments have lower risks, but all investing involves risk.

How To Get Started:

I was once teaching a group of new doctors about basic investing principles—doctors have to learn this information on their own since medical school does not cover it. One of the doctors asked how to "get started." I told her to go online or call an investment firm/brokerage and follow the steps she was given on the phone. Her follow up question was, "Ok, but how do you get started?" I went through it again, and she still didn't quite seem to understand. I obviously was not being clear enough or there was some other disconnect. Now, to avoid this confusion, I hand out these "Get Started" directions to my basic investing principles classes.

The stock exchange is a closed system, so you must use a certified/recognized brokerage account to buy and sell stocks. Although you don't need an actual flesh-and-blood broker, you must at least have an account with an approved brokerage firm and run your trades (purchases or sales of investments) through their system. You can choose from brokerage firms. I am going to use Fidelity for this example, simply because it is one of the largest and I have experience with them. Fidelity also has a large customer service department available should questions arise with your account. In my experience, some of the heavily advertised discount brokerage firms have less than adequate customer service to help you work through customer service issues.

1. Go to https://www.fidelity.com
2. Click the "open an account" button.
3. Select the type of account you want to open.
4. Determine the minimum deposit required to open the account.
5. Answer a series of questions about your account.
6. Fill out the information on the account.
7. If you are under eighteen, you need to involve a parent or guardian and must choose a youth or a custodial account. FYI, they want your Social Security information for tax purposes, so you won't be able to lie about your age. The federal government requires this, not just Fidelity. Your

parents will have to enter their information as well.

8. You should also look for any special sales or promotions, such as those where the brokerage firm gives you extra money for using their firm.

9. Set up your online brokerage account.

10. You can also make an appointment and go into your local Fidelity office where they will walk you through this entire process—they will likely do it for you if you are polite.

11. Complete your online brokerage account and transfer at least the minimum amount (currently $100 but this is subject to change).

12. Begin your stock trades online!

Cheat Codes:

Stocks represent partial ownership in a corporation, which allows the stockholder to share in the company profits or the assets if the company should dissolve—in proportion to their ownership. Stock investors make money primarily in two ways. A stock pays dividends (a payment of the company profits to its owners) and/or the company becomes more valuable over time making the investor a profit when the investment is sold. Only corporations can create stocks. To be able to remain a corporation, it must follow specific rules and accounting practices outlined by the SEC. Stocks are bought and sold on an open stock market called a stock exchange.

Stocks are created when a private company wants to expand, typically when the company has more potential orders than products to sell. The company works with a bank to create the necessary funds to expand. In exchange for those funds, partial ownership is given (in the form of stocks or shares) to the bank. The bank, in turn, sells the stocks on the open stock exchange to make a potential profit. To create and sell stocks, a company must follow a very specific federally mandated legal structure that requires the new corporation to elect a board of directors. The board of directors, in turn, selects the senior corporation's managers.

Investors face two large categories of risk when purchasing stocks. Systematic risk, which is a temporary downturn of the economy that broadly impacts most stocks dragging their value lower (at least temporarily). The second broad category of risk an investor may encounter is called non-systematic risk, which is a poorly run company or an entire industry that is struggling. Short-term traders lose money the majority of the time and generally quit within three years. Those who win in the stock market are usually those who buy and hold stocks for long periods of time.

To get started investing, go to an approved brokerage firm and open an account. If you are under 18 years of age, you will have to work with a parent or guardian.

Up Next:
If you want to learn how to bring all the information together into an easy to use, comprehensive investing plan, keep reading.

How The Stock Market Works Education Game:
A very popular game and educational tool in high schools and colleges. https://www.howthemarketworks.com

17

A Simple Investing Strategy Wins the Money Game

"Don't look for the needle in the haystack. Just buy the haystack!" — **John Bogle**

Bogle was a visionary who invented the index mutual fund. When marketing the index fund, he was widely ridiculed and called irresponsible for selling these investments to average investors. An index is a theoretical grouping of investments (such as stocks or bonds) that track a specific sector of our economy, such as the financial sector (banks and finance companies) or the building sector. One of the most famous indexes is the Dow Jones Industrial Average (simply called the Dow), which tracks large industrial stocks.

Index mutual funds, also known as index funds, have been proven to be superior to managed mutual funds because the fees are so much lower and managed funds can't overcome that advantage. Stock prices now move together more than ever before because of the widespread use of index funds. Stock Market index funds are now the most popular investment in history. Bogle was a multi-millionaire before his death in 2019.

Would you like to be financially independent, quit the traditional grind of a 9-to-5 job, and travel around the country? Steve and Courtney did just that! Read their amazing story below:

Steve and Courtney became financially independent and retired from their normal jobs when they were thirty-five years old. Now, they only work at the things they have a passion for and want to do in order to create income streams.

Steve was an IT worker and Courtney was an engineer. About ten years before leaving their traditional jobs they decided they wanted to become financially independent and retire. The couple created goals, developed a plan, and then moved forward to achieve their objectives. The first thing they did was cut their expenses by 70% and invested everything that was left. When they had accumulated about $850K, the couple left their traditional jobs. From that point on they followed the 4% rule of withdrawal, which means they only withdraw from their investment accounts 4% annually (less when the stock market is down) and now they have accumulated a net worth of around $12 million.[1] Of course, they utilize their side-gig income streams to supplement or reduce their investment withdrawals.

A key part of their plan involved both Steve and Courtney maxing out their company's 401Ks (company retirement account) and Individual Retirement Accounts (IRA). With this simple strategy (along with drastic spending cuts), they accomplished their wealth building goals. Now the couple travels around the USA in an Airstream and work from the trailer at various projects they have chosen, which is their dream life.[2]

If you want to be like Steve and Courtney—or like my wife and I, who have a similar story—you will need an investing plan.

It is a lucky coincidence that the most profitable plan for you to pursue as a young investor is also the easiest approach to investing!

In addition to the essential concepts we have already covered in this book, a simple investing plan involves four basic actions:

1. Continue investing over your lifetime (called dollar cost averaging).

2. Create a mix of different investments to ensure diversity (owning many different investments).

3. Max out a variety of tax-favored accounts (401K, IRAs), as your primary investment vehicle(s).

4. Keep investing costs as low as possible by using broad-based index funds (mutual funds that mirror all the stocks in a specific sector of our economy), which are typically safer for the average investor. See more about index funds below.

With these four actions, you can easily create a successful investing strategy. You can learn a lot more about investing, and it is essential you keep educating yourself, but these simple steps will move you well down the road to financial abundance. Now let's cover these terms in a little more detail.

Dollar Cost Averaging:

Cost averaging is a universally accepted investment strategy. It involves buying a set amount of investments regularly, such as every week, biweekly, or monthly. The purchases are made by routing some of your income from every paycheck straight into your investment account to buy assets, which helps smooth out the cost of your investments over time. For example, if you use a set dollar amount to purchase an index fund each month, this creates a situation where you end up buying more shares of the index fund when the market is down and less when it is higher. Over time, this strategy has proven to be an extremely successful investing principle that leads to great profits.

SIMPLE INVESTING PLAN

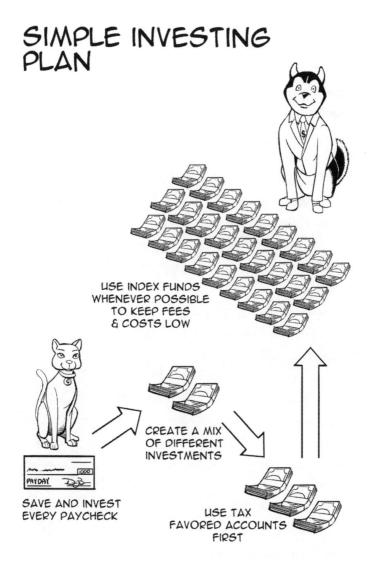

USE INDEX FUNDS WHENEVER POSSIBLE TO KEEP FEES & COSTS LOW

CREATE A MIX OF DIFFERENT INVESTMENTS

SAVE AND INVEST EVERY PAYCHECK

USE TAX FAVORED ACCOUNTS FIRST

This strategy ignores market direction (market currently headed up or down) and timing (trying buy and sell stocks to maximize your profit based on what you think the market will do in the near future). It doesn't matter what the price of a stock might be on any particular month. Over the long term, at least so far in recorded history, the overall direction of the stock market has been up. What is expensive today will likely seem inexpensive compared to its cost 10 to 15 years from now.

Investment Diversity:

Diversity in investing implies you own several different asset classes (stocks, bonds, real estate, etc.) and possibly several different investment subclasses. For example, you own stocks from different types of companies and corporate and government bonds. Also, you might purchase residential and commercial real estate. The examples are nearly endless.

> Investment diversity can be considered the most valuable investing principle after compounding interest!

Diversity increases investment safety and improves overall performance over the long haul. The investing principle behind this concept is that every investment class (type of investment) has specific downsides and upsides that do better or worse when certain economic conditions occur. For example, during a recession (a broad downturn in economic activity), large corporation stocks don't typically perform very well. At the same time stocks are faltering, however, bonds tend to do well. By owning a variety of investment classes, no matter which investment is doing well at a particular moment, you already own that investment. The favored investment is already hard at work earning you money. Diversity is a basic investing "best practice" that has been time tested and mathematically proven to work better than being invested in only one or two different types of assets.

> You call your collection of diverse investments your portfolio or your investment portfolio.

Here are three examples of asset investment classes and how you might mix them to maximize your profits and increase investing safety.

Owning stocks or stock mutual funds (a holding company that owns a variety of stocks) is considered a more aggressive investment than owning bonds (or bond mutual funds). The goal of diversification is to primarily mix stocks and bonds together to increase safety/decrease risk. For example, if stocks start doing very poorly—which happens regularly— bonds and other investments tend to counteract or at least slow the fall in value of your overall investment portfolio.

Aggressive To Conservative Portfolio Chart:

	Agressive	Moderate	Conservative
Stocks	80%	60%	30%
Bonds	15%	30%	50%
Cash	5%	10%	20%

Source: https://intelligent.schwab.com/article/
determine-your-risk-tolerance-level[3]

The chart above contains approximations. People generally add a few more assets or investment classes as they build their investing knowledge. The younger the person, the more aggressive the portfolio mix because of the longer time period to make up any losses that periodically occur in investing. The more aggressive (higher percentage of stocks) your mix of investments, the greater a chance for larger profit, however, a higher risk brings with it a higher probability you might suffer a loss, up to and including your initial investment. Keep reading and studying to maximize your investing effectiveness.

Tax Favored Accounts:

At our house, we primarily used these three account types to build our fortune, which is also a great way for you to begin your journey to prosperity.

IRA: An Individual Retirement Account (IRA). You set up an IRA with a brokerage firm, bank or credit union and fund it entirely on your own without employer sponsorship or contributions. The money you invest into the account is tax deferred, meaning that the money you place in the account is not taxed before it is invested and grows tax free. It will be taxed at your normal income tax rate when you begin withdrawing the funds, which typically begins at age 59 ½ or later. How much you contribute to an IRA is not impacted by you or your employer's contributions to your company's 401K plan.

401K: A 401K is your employer sponsored tax-deferred account named after the IRS code that created it. To get this account up and running, contact the personnel department of your company and ask them to assist with the paperwork to start this plan. An employer's 401K traditionally allows you to contribute pre-tax dollars (called tax deferred because it is not taxed until you withdraw the money) to this plan directly from your paycheck. These accounts are popular because most employers will typically match some of the funds you route into this account, up to a certain percentage of your total pay.

AGGRESSIVE TO CONSERVATIVE INVESTMENT PORTFOLIOS

PORTFOLIO: TYPES AND PERCENTAGES OF INVESTMENTS IN YOUR ACCOUNT

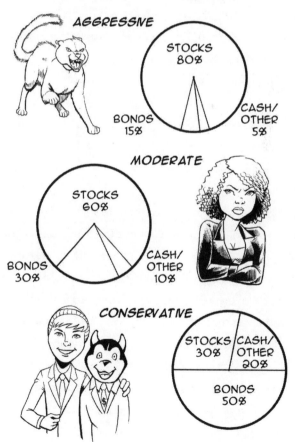

For example, some employers match up to 3% of your total pay, if you place it into the company's 401K plan. Use your payroll department to set up the direct deposit of your funds into this account, so there is no chance of spending your investment money on anything else.

Typically, when you are 59 1/2 year of age, you are permitted to begin withdrawing from this account without penalty. Any attempt to remove the funds before the proper age, however, is met with severe withdrawal and tax penalties. When you remove the funds from your 401K, you pay the income tax rate in place (the rate your annual income dictates) at the time of your withdrawal. Most employees can contribute up to $22,500 (as of 2023) a year into this type of account.

Most company 401K's now allow some investment choices within their plans. Usually, but not in every instance, the choices in company plans are limited. If possible, choose indexed mutual funds.

Important: If your employer does not match any funds you deposit into the company's sponsored 401K plan, skip to the ROTH IRA.

ROTH: The second type of account, a ROTH, is a special type of IRA. You will want to be sure to incorporate one into your own collection of investment accounts. You can set up this account by contacting a brokerage firm. A ROTH utilizes after-tax money you receive in your paycheck. You pay all normal income taxes on the money you use to fund your ROTH. The cool thing about a ROTH is that all the profits (and the after-tax-money you contributed) come to you completely tax free at age 59 1/2. You may also withdraw the money you invest into your Roth, tax free, anytime you wish (after 5 years). The profits you made in the account can only be accessed without significant penalties after you turn 59 1/2.

Most people are only allowed to defer $6,500 outside of 401K plan, therefore your contribution to a traditional IRA and your Roth IRA can total $6,500 (as of 2023). In other words, if you contribute $4,000 to a traditional IRA, you may only contribute $2,500 to a ROTH.

The 401K, the traditional IRA and the Roth will get you up and running. Just these three accounts should be more than adequate for the next few years.

Check the IRS site (irs.gov) for the latest rules governing these accounts.

Using Index Funds to Keep Investing Fees Low:

To understand what an index fund is and what it does, we first need to understand mutual funds. A professional manager hired by the fund uses the money generated by the sale of shares of the mutual fund to buy stocks, bonds, real estate and other investments to pursue the advertised strategy set by its shareholders.

In exchange for the fund's professional management, investors may pay a fee ranging on average from .75% to 1.5% annually, which means that a fund having a 1% fee will require an account holder with a balance of $100K to pay a mutual fund management fee of $1,000 annually whether your account earns or loses money. All fees are simply deducted from your account balance.

As you can see, mutual fund fees are significant and should always be considered before making any investment purchase.

OPEN AND USE
THESE ACCOUNTS FIRST

LEVEL 1
DOES YOUR EMPLOYER MATCH SOME OF YOUR DEPOSITS? IF THE ANSWER IS "NO", SKIP TO LEVEL 2

-EMPLOYER'S 401K
- PRE-TAX DOLLARS (NO TAXES UNTIL WITHDRAW)
- UP TO $20,500 ANNUALLY (2022)
- EMPLOYER MAY MATCH A CERTAIN PERCENTAGE OF THE $$ YOU INVEST.
*CAN BE WITHDRAWN AT AGE 59$^{1/2}$

LEVEL 2
$6000 TOTAL BETWEEN THESE 2 ACCOUNTS ALLOWED (2022)

TRADITIONAL IRA

- OPEN THESE ACCOUNTS AT A BROKERAGE FIRM
- YOU FUND THESE ACCOUNTS WITHOUT YOUR EMPLOYER'S HELP.

*YOU CAN WITHDRAW ROTH DEPOSITS AT ANY TIME, BUT PROFITS CAN ONLY BE WITHDRAWN AT AGE 59$^{1/2}$

ROTH IRA

PRE-TAX MONEY

* EXTRA TAXES AND PENALTIES APPLY FOR EARLY WITHDRAW

POST TAX ACCOUNT. MEANS YOU USE YOUR REGULAR PAY. NO TAXES DUE IF WITHDRAWN AFTER AGE 59$^{1/2}$.

People sometimes choose professionally managed mutual funds because they believe a professional manager can make them more money than they could make if they purchased indexed mutual funds on their own. Studies of long-term data have shown that although this is occasionally true, the vast majority of the time this is a false premise when the low fees of indexed mutual funds are considered.

Now, let's go into more detail regarding index mutual funds.

An index is a theoretical grouping of invest-
ments (such as stocks or bonds) that track a
sector of our economy, one of the most famous
indexes being the Dow Jones Industrial Average
(simply called the Dow).

Stock indexes track small to large companies, stocks, bonds, commodities, and other investments. The four most widely followed indexes in the U.S. are:

1. Standard and Poor's (The "S&P 500"): An index of America's 500 largest companies. The large companies are commonly called large caps which implies they have a large capitalization or large amount of net worth. A large cap generally has a net worth of over ten billion dollars.

2. Dow Jones Industrial Average (The "Dow"): An index of 30 larger companies that trade on the New York Stock Exchange, which is the most-quoted index in the world. Created by a news company, it remains popular today because it is considered a barometer of how our economy is doing.

3. Nasdaq Composite (The "NASDAQ"): A group of large tech companies. One of the top three indexes followed in the U.S.

4. Russell 2000: 2000 prominent small cap companies, though Wall Street's definition of small actually means the company has a value (capitalization) of over 3.8 billion.

Bond indexes are available for bonds issued by the U.S. federal, state, and local governments. Bond indexes also exist for corporate bonds or other countries' bonds. The U.S. Aggregate Bond Index is considered the overall bond index. It includes corporate bonds, U.S. Treasury bonds and some international bonds.

An index fund is a fund that attempts to exactly mirror a particular index, such as those listed above. Typically, this is a stock index like the Dow. An index fund has a large group of stocks or bonds that mimics the index it is dedicated to following.

Index fund investing has become the most popular method of investing in modern history.

Investors like index funds for two primary reasons:

1. Extremely low administration fees (typically .25% or lower)
2. Index funds typically outperform managed funds over the long haul.

In 2010 Andy and Nicole Hill realized that things had to change regarding their family's financial trajectory. The Hill family (Mom, dad and two kids) realized they had a negative $50,000 net worth. The debt they had accrued stemmed from school loans, a car payment, and a mortgage on the family home. To create a different reality, the couple set goals and took action! The first order of business was to pay off all their debt. The Hill family developed very successful side gigs and significantly increased their income. They also reduced spending and soon paid off their debts. Once the debts were paid off, they moved on to investing. Their primary investment vehicles were their company 401Ks, personal IRAs and Roths, which they promptly maxed-out. Inside of those *accounts, they primarily invested in index mutual funds (when they could) because they loved the low fees and fairly consistent performance. In 2020, Andy and Nicole reached their goal and became millionaires.*[4]

Cheat Codes:

The simple four-step investing plan initially involves regular deposits in tax deferred accounts including your employer's 401K, traditional IRA, and a Roth IRA. This will get you up and running to build the future of your dreams.

1. Invest every payday (dollar cost averaging)
2. Create investing/asset diversity
3. Max out a variety of tax-favored accounts
4. Use broad-based index funds

This plan is all you need to know for several years as you spend time reading and learning more about investing and creating financial abundance.

Up Next:

Of course, I haven't discussed the hottest new investment since the index fund. Keep reading to learn more about where cryptocurrency falls within your investing plan.

Stock Market Simulator Game — You Can Compete Against Others:

A stock market simulator game designed via a partnership with Fidelity Investments and the informational website Investopedia. com where you use virtual money and a simulation tool on your own or compete with others to determine who is the best. https://www.investopedia.com/simulator/

18

Cryptocurrency and NFTs: The Game's Secret Treasures or Traps?

"If you don't believe it or don't get it, I don't have the time to try to convince you, sorry." — **Satoshi Nakamoto, pseudonym of the inventor of cryptocurrency, whose real identity is not known even to this day**

True believers loudly proclaim that cryptocurrency will eventually conquer the earth and change everything! They believe it is only a matter of time before Bitcoin (or some other cryptocurrency) achieves world domination and takes its place as the top dog and other currencies fade away into oblivion. Yet, if you ask one of the true believers to explain Bitcoin, they may very well decline to do so. During my research, I frequently read comments like "You need to do the work to understand Bitcoin." This attitude is prevalent throughout the Bitcoin community, which can be almost like an elite club, inaccessible to the average non-techie.[1]

Currently, over 1,600 cryptocurrencies exist, and new ones are being created every day. Bitcoin is the largest and most popular cryptocurrency. The next largest cryptocurrency is Ethereum. Close behind these cryptocurrencies are Litecoin and Stellar Lumens and don't forget Dogecoin , which also has a large following. Which cryptocurrency will dominate? No one truly knows, even though every true believer has his or her heartfelt opinion. I liken cryptocurrency to the old VHS and Beta tape technology war (how movies used to be recorded/stored for home viewing). VHS eventually won the battle, taking around nine years to achieve market dominance. A few years later, however, VHS tapes lost the market to more-advanced video storage capabilities of DVDs and Blu-ray. Now all have been replaced by readily available on-demand streaming services. In short, cryptocurrency (pick your favorite one) is popular and cutting edge. It is my opinion that if one cryptocurrency wins, its dominance will be short-lived, and it will soon be replaced in our ever-advancing technological evolution.

If you think the above comparison is groundless, and crypto lovers surely will, I have evidence to support my view. Cryptocurrency is not a physical thing in space and time; it is just a data code - an encoded, multi-record data packet stored on a decentralized network. Cryptocurrency is a type of code that creates and then stores data on a ledger type file system called blocks, which is the blockchain technology that helps support cryptocurrency validation (to prevent fraud) and create the transparency processes. Each block is also encrypted or encoded with a secret code, making it extremely hard for unauthorized persons to access or hack—but not impossible. Additional uses for blockchain technology are now being explored and include mass data storage, notary services, crowdfunding, medical records storage and even a voting system.[2] It's hard to believe this technology will not be altered/improved in the near future.

BITCOIN IS CREATED BY AN ENCRYPTED DECENTRALIZED LEDGER CALLED BLOCKS

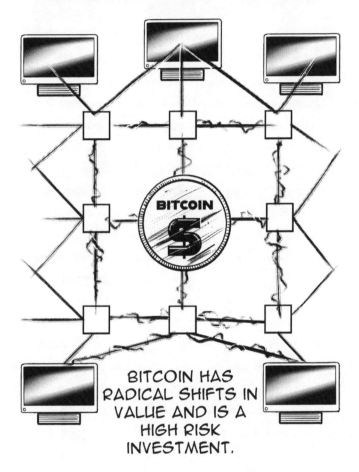

BITCOIN HAS RADICAL SHIFTS IN VALUE AND IS A HIGH RISK INVESTMENT.

Bitcoin and other cryptocurrencies have a history of wild volatility as an investment. In July 2021, the price of Bitcoin went from extreme lows to an amazingly high price of $69K per coin. Then the price dropped a full 40% in November 2021 to $33k. The price, as of

April 2023, is around $29K per coin. Given this extreme volatility, I rate the risk of investing in crypto as extremely high, even for a long-term investor (like you). I would limit my exposure to this volatility/risk by only owning a small percentage at most in my portfolio.

Normally I would give you a story about one or several Bitcoin investors becoming millionaires, as thousands were created by Bitcoins' meteoric rise in price, reported in headline after headline in early 2021. By 2022, however, thousands of Bitcoin millionaires were wiped out as the prices dropped like a heavy stone in a pond. Not only that, but those who brokered Bitcoins had to find another line of work. Also in 2022, Bitcoins were stolen for the first time by hacking the network in which the coins were stored. Networks that store bitcoins appear to be the weakest link in the chain.

FTX was a company that sold investments (called futures) that were tied to the future prices of various cryptocurrencies. FTX recently went bust and became insolvent. During the media storm that followed, media reported that the primary reason for the company's failure was gross mismanagement and a great deal of (not yet proven) fraud. Sam Bankman-Fried (founder and president of FTX) is currently under house arrest at his parents' home awaiting trial. This is a great reminder that despite laws, rules, and common decency, investment fraud is still alive and well in our society. This story is not unusual as people commit fraud in reference to investments with alarming regularity. The best protection is once again, diversity and investing knowledge.

Many young investors like Elizabeth Torres of Newark, Delaware, share a different opinion about cryptocurrency. Ms. Torres has a financial education background and has made it her mission to educate minorities and others in the area of building financial prosperity. She has created a variety of Facebook pages like Financial Literacy for Minorities, written articles and has several websites. Like me, she is heavily involved in educating people on the essential skills needed for financial literacy.

Torres believes it is normal for older people to view cryptocurrencies with suspicion, especially since they created the bulk of their nest eggs with traditional investments. That doesn't mean, however, that cryptocurrencies will not be a mainstream investment in the near future.[3] She believes crypto will evolve and increase in value. Crypto's current volatility is caused by its relative newness. She believes it will even out over time.

Torres' view does have some merit. For example, since Ukraine has been invaded by Russia, the traditional Ukrainian currency has become nearly worthless. People in that country now use crypto almost exclusively. This, in fact, supports the view that crypto has value separate from the financial system of any one nation. That is a powerful argument for holding at least some crypto.

At the same time this is going on, however, the Department of Labor warns investors that the crypto market's future remains uncertain and there is no agreement or standard regarding investment fundamentals in crypto due to its volatility. The Department also says evaluations of crypto vary widely and investing in them in a retirement portfolio can create serious problems down the road if crypto is devalued.[4]

Erik Finman of Post Falls, Idaho, made a deal with his parents to avoid college. Erik got them to agree that if he could become a millionaire by age eighteen, he could skip going to college. Erik was being pushed into going to college by his parents who were Stanford educated PhDs. School was not working for Erik and he hated it, which probably led one of his teachers to suggest that Erik drop out of school and work at McDonalds. Erik started his journey with a $1,000 his grandmother gave him. Erik bought and sold bitcoin and created several high-tech start-ups that he sold for a nice profit. Erik is now involved in technology company sales and is a multi-millionaire.[5]

Two ways to invest in cryptocurrency:

1. You cannot buy physical crypto coins as they do not exist in our physical world; they are an encoded data packet that is stored on a network. See "How Bitcoin Works for the Digitally Impaired" at FaulknerFinancialFreedom. com for step by step details to purchase a bitcoin.[6]

2. Purchase a mutual fund that trades in cryptocurrency futures. Futures means buying and selling on contracts based on the anticipated price of cryptocurrency. To further explain, you could buy shares of a mutual fund such as Grayscale Bitcoin Trust (GBTC) that invests in Bitcoin futures, which trades on all major US exchanges and can be bought at Fidelity and other brokerage firms. Similar mutual funds trade in a variety of cryptocurrency futures, which reduces the worry about which crypto will dominate in the future.

From blockchain technology sprung a similar type of digitally traded item of supposed value called an NFT (non-fungible token).

The term non-fungible implies you can't trade it for a like or similar item.

The concept of NFTs sounds way more complicated than it is. NFTs use the new blockchain technology to create original digital art, which is typically a picture, meme, GIF, game token in a video game or even a digital baseball card. Money is fungible. A dollar bill can be traded for another dollar bill without a loss or increase in value. They are like and similar. NFTs and other unique digital items cannot be traded for like and similar items. With an NFT, the value and beauty are contained solely within the eye of the beholder. When they were first introduced, NFTs were considered cutting edge. The original NFTs sold for a small fortune. After being out for a while, however, NFTs have come way down in value.

> Creators may embed a contract within an NFT, so if the artwork is resold, a piece of the sale is routed to the creator.

One of the primary criticisms of NFTs is that someone (anyone really) can copy the NFT artwork by doing a screenshot or taking a picture of it by some other means, although, they do not have the original file. Most of us likely do not care about having the original file, but that is not true in all cases. For example, commercial uses of NFTs include creating digital sports cards of players. Anyone can copy one, but it won't be an original digital card issued by the official company with the original blockchain code. For sports memorabilia collectors, obtaining an official card (original file that carries its own authentication) is a big deal. Also, another great commercial use of NFTs has been game tokens within video games. For example, a game token found or earned in a game could give the user a new skin (outfit) or new battle gear for their character.

No one can copy that token into their own game because the video environment is only set up to handle the digital tokens. The original token gives real value to gaming fans in this case.

*NFT*s ARE DIGITAL ART

Twelve-year-old Nyla Hayes was a burgeoning artist when she and her mom researched NFTs and learned how to make them. Nyla went on to create the extremely popular art series, Long Neckies, that depict important, transformational women in the world who are portrayed in a very particular artistic style. In each portrait her women have long necks that she says comes from her love of Brontosaurus dinosaurs as a child. Art critics say her designs with the long-necked women portray them elegantly. It also doesn't hurt that she portrays a diverse group of women who have influenced history and the future. Selling her art made Nyla a multi-millionaire with significant professional opportunities in the art field.[7]

I believe the new NFT technology has a bright future. The use of NFTs is starting to penetrate the music industry. Musicians are choosing to skip the normal corporate music release structure that pays them only pennies on dollars earned and instead, are releasing their own music as NFTs. This has the music companies like Spotify scrambling to block the use of NFTs (so far entirely unsuccessful) or incorporate the technology into their sales strategy.

As an investment or in the resale market with an eye toward profit, the value of an NFT is very much dependent on the value a potential customer might place upon it—just like all other art.

You buy cryptocurrency and NFTs entirely at your own risk. Cryptocurrency, like Bitcoin, provides you with zero legal protections. Payments are not reversible. If you are ripped off, lose your crypto wallet code, lose access to the NFT or your crypto is stolen on the network, you can expect zero help in recovering your financial losses. One final comment:

Cryptocurrency is not legal tender in the vast majority of countries.

Cheat Codes:

Cryptocurrency functions on an encoded and decentralized network that creates and stores blocks. Blocks can be likened to records (entries) on a database or a ledger. Over 1,600 cryptocurrencies currently exist, and new ones are being created every day. Bitcoin is the largest and most popular cryptocurrency. The next largest cryptocurrency is Ethereum, then Litecoin, Stellar Lumens and don't forget Dogecoin. Many uses for blockchain technology are just being explored, such as uneditable ledgers. Finally, NFTs (non-fungible tokens) also utilize blockchain technology to create unique digital files—like artwork for example. The value, like art, relies solely in the eye of the beholder. Businesses, however, are developing several commercial uses for NFTs that involve collectables and game rewards. No one has to accept crypto, and it is even illegal to use in some countries. Proceed into the blockchain arena with extreme caution as the prices fluctuate radically.

Up Next:

Would you like your own chance to create a very successful side gig? Read the things you need to know in the next chapter.

Bitcoin Blockchain Game:

You create blockchains and earn cryptocurrency in this game.
https://apps.apple.com/us/app/blockchain-to-bitcoin/
id1323596514

19

Love Your Side Gig to Effectively Play the Game

"If you do something just for the money, the love of it will soon die. If you do something you love, then the money is secondary, but it will come a lot easier and it will last longer." — **Bruce Lee, film star, modern philosopher, and breakthrough martial artist, who built a huge martial arts following and movie fan base. At the time of Lee's death in 1973 he was a multi-millionaire**

In Chapter 7, we talked about the importance of creating alternative sources of income to increase your annual income, your financial resilience, and your overall net worth. If you start thinking, "Man, that sure is a lot of work time," who could blame you? Side gig burnout is a very real thing and it happens all the time.

The best way to overcome the obstacle of side gig burnout is to love your side gig.

If the activity is fun or engaging, then it seems less like work and more like a hobby. The website sidehustlenation.com reports that 45% of working-age Americans actively have a side hustle, with that number rising to 50% among millennials. While only 50% of those surveyed reported they loved their day jobs, 76% reported loving what they do for their side gigs. The website also reported that most Americans with a side gig make somewhere between $200 (average) and $1,122 (statistical median) each month. The average time spent on a side gig ranged from 11 to 16 hours monthly, and this usually returned somewhere in the neighborhood of $16 to $23 hourly.[1]

Countless ways exist to earn extra money. For example, you can create informational products to sell. Some people have made big money in this field. The same skills needed to build a good social media following are needed for marketing your informational products.

Kat Norton, who is known as Miss Excel on TikTok and Instagram, worked for a consulting firm helping banks package, underwrite and then sell loans and other contractual receivables (interest-paying investments) for years. In her spare time, however, Norton loved developing Microsoft Excel courses for beginners. She liked Excel and had mastered this program while attending business college. Her job at the consulting firm was entirely unfulfilling. It was so bad that she quit the job, and then began trying to figure out what to do next. In a brainstorming session with a friend, she got the idea of posting entertaining online videos on TikTok and Instagram about time-saving Excel shortcuts. The videos are put to music and she dances in the foreground while the Excel shortcut is shown above her. In other videos, she does funny skits with friends.

The videos are recorded and produced on her iPhone without any special equipment.

What separates her from other TikTok and social media influencers is that she uses her social media videos as a sales tool only. The videos are the primary driver for selling her online software training courses. To date, Kat has generated over $1 million in gross sales.[2]

Selling informational products is the not the only way to make extra money. Reselling new or used items is one of the surest ways to create extra income. Buying and selling merchandise that you have a preexisting interest in, or already know something about because of a particular hobby or activity, can be a good fit. For example, if you love video games, then it will be easier for you to buy and sell these items since you already know something about them and what vintage or new video games currently sell for. The same would be true for vintage clothing, fishing equipment, Native American arrowheads, or comic books. It might be better to first sell some unused items or clothing you have around the house to generate start-up cash and to see if you like this type of business.

Buying and selling used or repackaged new items will allow you to tap into an online global market expected to hit over four trillion customers in 2023, with 300 million of those shoppers living in the U.S. Reselling has unlimited potential and can easily develop into a very important side income for those who have an interest in that business.[3]

You can resell nearly anything, but at the time of this writing, it is extremely popular to resell brand-name clothing, antiques and electronics. More importantly, it has also become very popular to buy used and new clothing items online to save money. The good news is, by reselling used items or flipping new merchandise, social media/online sellers can provide products directly to this market and bypass traditional sales channels that drain much of the profitability away from sellers.

The most popular sites to resell merchandise include:

- Facebook Marketplace
- depop.com
- poshmark.com
- swap.com
- ThredUp.com
- ebay.com
- Craigslist.org
- Amazon (for resale of new merchandise)

Each site has pros and cons, including fee structures, shipping policies and specific sales strategies. The more expensive the item you resell, the more room there is for markup and profit.

Some sites specialize in certain items. For example, Depop and Poshmark specialize in brand-name clothing. Amazon specializes in reselling new merchandise called retail arbitrage, where buyers purchase new items in one market and sell them for a profit in a different market. Retail arbitrage is an entirely different endeavor than reselling used items online. Poshmark has a great easy-to-use app to support your reselling efforts.

Online reselling involves a number of important skills, including photography. Good photos are one of the keys to making frequent sales. Luckily, plenty of online instruction videos will show you how to photograph objects in an appealing way. Understanding the price of the items you are buying and selling is also relevant. Buying and selling higher-value items comes with higher rewards, but also a greater risk if you get stuck with high-value items that you can't resell.

LOVE YOUR SIDE GIG

- TRY SELLING UNUSED STUFF YOU ALREADY
  HAVE TO GENERATE YOUR STARTUP CASH.
- DON'T USE PROFITS TO
  INCREASE YOUR SPENDING.
- USE TALENTS & SKILLS YOU ALREADY HAVE.
- CREATE A SIDE GIG RELATED
  TO YOUR INTERESTS.
- RESELLING ITEMS OFFERS SAFEST ROUTE TO
  SUCCESS & ALMOST ANYONE CAN DO IT.
- BUY AT A LOW PRICE.
  SELL AT A HIGHER PRICE.

Although it can be fun, reselling is still a business, and it is not a good fit for the unorganized.

You must be analytical and disciplined to be successful at keeping track of your inventory, which includes recording the history of your merchandise such as purchase price, profit/loss and the paperwork needed for proper tax preparation. You must also be sure you are actually making a profit once you consider the following costs:

- Price of the item verses the margin (your profit) on the item upon resell
- Website fees
- Shipping fees
- Shipping supplies
- Time spent finding the item
- Time spent putting the item in inventory
- Photographing and describing an item in a post to sell it
- Time involved in shipping

If you are making below minimum wage once you add up the time you spent, you might consider changing your business model, finding another product or finding another side gig to pursue. Successful business resellers frequently figure out an average of their per-item costs (cost of goods sold), and can apply it on the fly to any item they consider purchasing and its potential profitability.

JV Orvitz of Brooklyn, New York, started out day-trading stocks. He lost money, so he searched around for something he could buy and sell with adequate profit margins. He started buying T-shirts for two dollars from thrift shops and reselling them for ten dollars. This strategy was profitable, but he felt he needed to find something to resell with higher margins. He was looking on eBay for things that cost in the $500 to $1,000 range when he came across sneaker. He started reselling sneakers *and found he was able to create huge margins by purchasing high end, popular brands cheaply and then reselling them. After only a few successful and surprisingly quick resells, he was hooked. Now he reports that he creates an income of $10,000 a month. He was able to quit his job and now resells full time. Using his forward momentum, he now has his own website where he resells the sneakers and just wrote a book about his experience. As an interesting side note, he says he does not maintain an inventory listing because his turnover is so quick.*[4]

Whatever side gig interests you, paying taxes on the income you make is an absolute legal requirement. It is entirely up to you to maintain the records you require to determine your exact tax liability. A simple Excel spreadsheet can handle most of these needs, along with saving all receipts and records. Recent lower thresholds for reporting your earnings to the IRS has slightly changed bookkeeping practices. Your tax rate is dependent upon your financial situation and is beyond the scope of this book. It is essential, however, to make sure you maximize your profit while always complying with all IRS tax requirements. Trying to file your taxes without adequate bookkeeping will quickly become a nightmare, not to mention the chaos you will encounter when you try to respond to any IRS inquiries without the needed paperwork.

If you are not great at being analytical and are more the creative type, becoming a social media influencer might be more up your alley. An influencer builds a following on social media platforms by communicating with an audience who is interested in the subject matter the influencer presents. The influencer builds a reputation for knowledge and expertise in a specific subject or field or is followed for entertainment purposes. Part of an influencer's job is to locate sponsors who are willing to pay for them to introduce products or brands to their social media followers, raising awareness of the product or brand and hopefully increasing the sponsor's sales.

THE BUSINESS OF YOUR BUSINESS

- TRACK YOUR INVENTORY

- MAINTAIN GOOD BUSINESS RECORDS

- KEEP ALL RECEIPTS & SALES SLIPS

- TRACK HOW MUCH PROFIT YOU MADE ON EACH ITEM YOU SELL

- RECORD ALL CUSTOMER E-MAILS FOR FUTURE SALES

- LEARN EXCEL & USE IT TO KEEP BUSINESS BOOKS/ RECORDS

- IRS WILL WANT TO SEE YOUR RECORDS

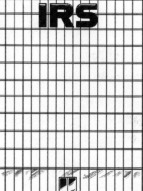

It was previously thought that only those with huge followings could influence followers or generate sales for companies and their products. Recently, however, even those with small followings (micro influencers) are now being sought by some advertisers. This requires you to understand your audience and what products interest them. Social media platforms popular for influencers today include:

- TikTok
- Instagram
- Facebook
- YouTube
- LinkedIn
- Blogs or Vlogs

Many people want to try their hand at becoming a popular influencer on social media. Although the process of becoming popular might seem easy to consumers, I assure you it is not. For example, the first job of a potential influencer is to build an audience. To build an audience requires expert-level communication and marketing skills along with an ability to create engaging short films. Creating engaging content is both an art and science. Some people have a gift for it, but it may be a challenge to come up with engaging content on a regular basis.

For example, Maggie Thurman, who started as an influencer on TikTok as a high school senior, has regular meetings with her family to come up with ideas for videos. She also has meetings with advertisers to discuss if and how their products will fit into her brand and her videos.[5]

Bella Poarch earned five million dollars last year through social media influencing videos, endorsements, and content creation.

Poarch is a great example of how you can overcome your past if you are determined, have talent, and an unstoppable drive despite the odds being stacked against you.[6] Bella came from a very troubled background in the Philippines and was adopted as a child. She then immigrated with her adopted family to Texas. Unfortunately, she suffered significant child abuse in her adopted home and has the scars to prove it. As soon as she could, she escaped her home life and joined the Navy. After serving a tour in the armed forces and getting her feet under her, she made a funny TikTok video of herself lip syncing a short segment of a Millie B song, M To The B. This video exploded and went viral. She then created more engaging content, and her audience grew exponentially. She now has 87 million followers and is the 3rd most followed account on TikTok. Bella used her forward momentum to release a single (song) called Build-a-Bitch, *and it placed No. 56 on the Billboard Pop Chart. She also received several MTV VMA nominations for her song. She has appeared in several music videos and has collaborated with top music industry perform-ers. Also, Poarch is a gamer and has appeared on several eSports videos and sometimes livestreams her sessions.[7]*

Many horror stories exist about people who failed as in-fluencers on social media. Not only were these people unable to build the following they wanted, but they went into serious debt because they had no sponsors and no income. These new influencers tried to purchase more exposure on the various plat-forms but still failed to increase their popularity or views. Many of them were forced to pay back the debt they ran up (on credit cards) for this additional exposure by working at a regular job and making payments.

SOCIAL MEDIA INFLUENCER TALENTS & SKILLS

SKILLS:

- BEING COMFORTABLE ON CAMERA

- SHORT VIDEO PRODUCTION

- DIGITAL MARKETING

- WRITTEN SALES SCRIPTS OR "COPYWRITING"

TALENT REQUIREMENTS:

- CREATIVITY

- IMAGINATION

- ABILITY & DESIRE TO ENTERTAIN OTHERS

I write personal finance and motivational articles that I post at *FaulknerFinancialFreedom.com*. Like all the other creative gigs, offering a quality product and finding readers and followers were my first goals. My ability to find regular readers is entirely dependent upon my ability to create engaging, quality content. People can spend their entire lives learning and improving their writing skills, just as you can spend your life striving within the art of short-video production or communication. The key is to create engagement with your audience. The next goal is to find companies that will pay you to promote their products using ads or links you can feature on your site.[8]

I am not a fan of the gig apps like Favor or Doordash that allow you to get approved as a contractor and jump right into work because they are essentially bringing your customers to you. It seems like the more popular ones have your share of the profits squeezed down to the bare minimum. Still, many people swear by various gig apps and love working for them. One of the primary attractions is that gig app contractors can set their own schedules and jump on whenever they have free time. Examples of gig apps range from chauffeuring people who need a ride, to doing tasks for people such as offering dog walking and sitting services.

Cheat Codes:

A full 45% of working-age Americans have a side hustle, with that number rising to 50% among millennials. Most people who engage in a successful side hustle love doing it. The average time spent on a side gig ranges from eleven to sixteen hours per month, and usually brings in about $16 to $23 per hour in income. Reselling new or used items is one of the most popular and surest ways to create extra income with minimal physical labor. Buying and selling used or repackaged new items will allow you to tap into an online global market that is expected to hit over four trillion customers in 2023. Reselling profit margins are extremely important- small profit margins may not be worth your trouble. The more expensive an item, the greater the opportunity you have to make a profit but also carries a greater risk of loss if you cannot resell the item. Social media is a great route to creating income if you can become popular.

Two primary ways exist to utilize social media in business. The first way is to use it to generate sales for the products you make or resell. The second most common way to use social media is to become a popular influencer and endorse products or influence others to try them. There is a lot more to becoming popular on a social media platform than meets the eye. For example, you must be good at communication, marketing, content creation and videography. Most people who attempt to find success in the arena do not succeed in becoming an influencer.

Up Next:

We have discussed many financial topics in this book. If you have stayed with me until now, you know way more than most people about building a sound and secure financial life. In the next chapter, you will learn how all these concepts fit together to create the life of your dreams.

Online Game:

Could you make a living using only the gig economy? Play this game and find out! https://ig.ft.com/uber-game/

20

Master List of Cheat Codes to Win Your Money Game

"It's up to us to choose whether we win or lose, and I choose to win." — Mary J. Blige, American Grammy-winning singer, songwriter, actress and producer; sold over 50 million albums, accumulated 9 platinum albums, 8 Grammy awards, 32 Academy Award nominations and 2 Golden Globe nominations. Blige is believed to have a net worth of over $20 million after growing up in a housing project in Yonkers, New York

When you are in your forties, you'll get out of bed when you are ready to get up. Why? Because you no longer need a nine-to-five job. You'll have some coffee and check your phone to see how much money you made. You'll learn that your investments are up and did well for you! Your money is working very hard for you; It goes out and usually makes more money for you no matter what you are doing or not doing on any particular day.

This chapter contains lists you can quickly reference to determine whether you understand all the vital concepts we covered and have the necessary knowledge required to succeed in your own Money Game.

Most people, sadly, choose debt slavery over prosperity because of the following:

- They believe that finances are boring because they do not yet understand the impact money will have upon their quality of life.

- They were taught next to nothing about money management and even less about building prosperity, so they have no idea why it is so important.

- They don't yet understand the Money Game is a game everyone must play! There are no exceptions or alternatives to playing the Money Game. The game has few do-overs and no extra lives. We must all eventually lie in the financial bed we created from the consequences of our actions.

- They don't yet have any idea how much money will dominate their entire life's story.

- Most young people were never taught that money equals freedom. The more money you have, the more freedom you get. Also, the more financially upward momentum you create and nurture, the better you will do financially.

- No one explained to them that being financially secure is almost always an active choice. You must consciously set goals, create a plan, and then take action to enact your plan. If you fail to do this, you end up following the default path of consumerism and debt slavery.

- They don't yet understand they will have to step outside the cultural box in which they were raised to create prosperity—a difficult shift in thinking for so many people.
  - ° There is no reason to take on crippling school debt. Society's core structure has shifted, yet our education related customs have remained static and are no longer serving us. A full 85% of millennials who created student debt now regret doing so!
  - ° Most people with school debt spend half their income to pay their school loans, keeping them in poor financial condition for an entire lifetime. Education is essential, but school debt is the Money Game's deadly trap.
- No one told them the pursuit of money is not evil! We are not hurting anyone else by using our talents, saving, planning, and then investing. After all, you can't help the poor by becoming one of them!
- No one explained to them that money is no guarantee of happiness, however, a lack of money will bring you almost certain misery. Choose security and happiness!
- No one told them that failing to save and invest will create significant regrets and money anxiety later in life.
- Most people do not know the Money Game's time clock will not give you enough time to learn every financial lesson by experience. Study and learn about money instead of making mistakes that are difficult and time consuming to correct.
- Most young people have no idea they should discuss financial goals with potential romantic partners before cohabitating or marrying. Cohabitation with a partner could create significant conflict due to clashing values and

goals that don't mesh. If you and your significant other are not both on the same page with creating prosperity, it is very unlikely to happen.

- The vast majority of people have never been taught that nothing can stop them from succeeding unless they give it permission to do so!

Six Reasons to Believe You Can Win the Money Game:

1. People who grew up in very poor families become wealthy every day. Our past gives us a point of view or a perspective on life, however, our past does not define us. Our past does not have to be our future. We are always more than our history! More than 21 million full-fledged millionaires are in the U.S. right now![1] Every year, over two million people in the U.S. become new millionaires, and the vast majority made their own money and did not inherit it.[2]

2. The well-traveled path to becoming financially independent involves the mastery of the five skill-based steps:
   a. Setting goals
   b. Creating income
   c. Budgeting your income
   d. Saving first and paying bills after you save
   e. Investing regularly and increasing your contribution annually or semi-annually

3. Humans are the only beings on earth who have the opportunity to imagine and then choose their own destiny. Don't squander this unique and amazing superpower!

4. You now understand the personal cost to pay for the time, effort and persistence needed to build prosperity and upward financial momentum. This cost, however,

is much less than the cost of debt slavery. For example, studies have shown a strong link between debt, unhappiness, and depression.

5. You realize the path to prosperity is controlled by your efficiency in converting your earned wages into assets that produce an income. Essentially, you are creating a golden goose that will lay golden eggs. Once established, your goose will provide you income forever. Once you understand this, your path becomes clearer.

6. If you make prosperity a goal and work on it consistently, you are very likely to succeed. Barriers may temporarily block your progress, but nothing can stop you unless you give up.

Simple Investing Plan that Will Win Your Money Game:

1. Send money each month (like a monthly bill you absolutely must pay) to your investment/brokerage accounts. Try to use direct deposit whenever possible.

2. Increase the amount you invest annually or semi-annually (as often as possible).

3. Create a diverse portfolio of investments, composed primarily of stock and bond index mutual funds.

4. Mix your stock and bond index funds to a level that provides you comfort.

5. Monitor your progress.

When you choose prosperity and set goals, you will need an action plan to achieve that outcome. One of the tools we use to monitor where we stand and our progress is our net worth. Compare your current net worth with where you want to be, then check your progress regularly. Have regular goal meetings with your partner.

To determine your net worth now:

- All Assets - All Liabilities = Net Worth

5 LEVELS TO WIN THE MONEY GAME

5. INVEST

4. SAVE

3. BUDGET

2. GENERATE INCOME

1. SET GOALS

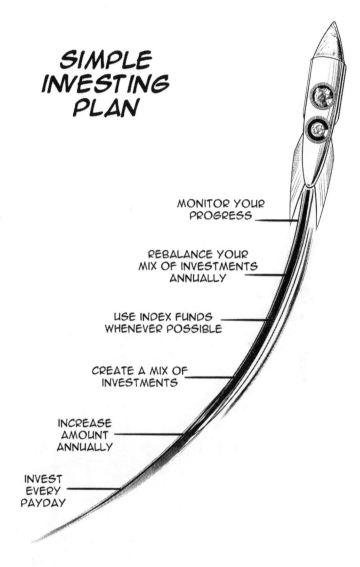

SIMPLE INVESTING PLAN

MONITOR YOUR PROGRESS

REBALANCE YOUR MIX OF INVESTMENTS ANNUALLY

USE INDEX FUNDS WHENEVER POSSIBLE

CREATE A MIX OF INVESTMENTS

INCREASE AMOUNT ANNUALLY

INVEST EVERY PAYDAY

Online Game:

Try different investment strategies and check the results twenty years in the future with this computer simulation game.

https://buildyourstax.com

A List of Quotes to Inspire You on Your Journey

"The only limit to the height of achievements is the reach of your dreams and your willingness to work for them." — Michelle Obama, First Lady of the 45th president, lawyer, writer, and activist for American health

"I find that the harder I work, the more luck I seem to have." — Thomas Jefferson, a founding father of our country and third U.S. president

"Believe you can, and you are halfway there." — Theodore Roosevelt, 26th president, Nobel Prize winner, self-made multi-millionaire, soldier, and adventurer

Glossary of Terms

401K: A tax-deferred employer-sponsored retirement account, named after the Internal Revenue Service (IRS) code that created it. The employer may match some of the funds the employee contributes. Typically, an employee can contribute up to $20K into this plan. (The contribution amount changes annually so check IRS.gov for the current amount.) You may not withdraw from this account without penalties and fees until you are at least fifty-nine and one-half years old or other special circumstances (defined in the code) occur. When you withdraw funds, these funds are taxed at your current income tax rate.

50/30/20 Budget: A budget in which 50% of your gross pay goes to fixed expenses like rent and car payments, 30% goes to variable expenses each month and 20% is routed directly to your savings or investment accounts.

Actuarial: Professionals who assess financial risk based upon statistics, probabilities, and economics. Actuarial data models are used by insurance companies and credit bureaus among many other companies.

Adjusted Gross Income (AGI): Your total income minus specific tax-deductible income, such as a 401K contribution, and expenses such as certain business expenses. AGI is less than your gross income.

Administrative Fee or Management Fee: The fee you are charged for having a professional stockbroker manage your investments. This charge covers salaries, bonuses and other personnel-related costs needed to manage the fund. Also, *see Expense Ratio.*

Aging Your Money: You use money you saved from prior paychecks to pay this month's bills and not living paycheck to paycheck.

Annual Percentage Rate (APR): The interest rate plus all the fees rolled into a percentage for a loan, allowing you to make loan comparisons.

Annual Report: A report required by the Securities and Exchange Commission (SEC) that explains a corporation's financial status, market share, the year's activities and their view of the corporation's future. Current shareholders and potential investors read these reports thoroughly to determine the company's risk and the potential future rewards (also, *see Quarterly Reports*).

Appreciation: An asset (investment) becomes more valuable over time. It is the opposite of depreciation, which is when something becomes less valuable over time.

Asset: Item of value that can be resold, such as land. It can also be something that produces income for additional value for its owner over time--such as a bond.

Asset Class: A group of investments that are similar in nature and have the same characteristics. They also trade in the same financial market and have the same set of rules they must follow issued by the government. Large asset classes include stocks, bonds, real estate, etc.

Auto Title Loans: A loan that uses your car's title as collateral (something you agree to forfeit to the lender if you don't pay your loan). You must own your car and have its title in order to use it as collateral. In the case of auto title loans, the borrower is charged huge fees on top of extremely high interest rates—such as 300% APR.

Automated Clearing House Network (ACH): A network for electronically moving funds between bank accounts in various banking institutions. It is considered a safe way to transfer money or pay bills. For example, the system handles direct deposits or monthly transfer of funds for routine bills that are pulled directly from a customer's account.

Automated Teller Machine (ATM) Card: An ATM card is used at ATM machines to check your account balance, make withdrawals and deposits and other basic banking functions. Some ATMs will charge you a fee for using an ATM that is not in your bank or credit union's network.

Automatic Bill Pay: Using your bank or credit union, you can have your routine bill payments automatically paid. You can fill out online forms with merchants, vendors, mortgage companies or your bank/credit union so routine payments are removed each month from your checking or savings account. By automating your routine bill payments, you can skip the monthly chore of remembering to pay bills by a certain date and risk forgetting to pay a bill. Of course, you must account for these payments (withdrawals) from your bank account and maintain an adequate balance to cover the payments. Failure to do so will result in bank fees.

Bank: A commercial, for-profit business that provides a variety of financial services to its customers (depositors). A bank accepts your deposits, keeps your money safe, allows withdrawals by writing checks or permitting electronic fund transfers in and out of the account. Banks also loan money to their customers and to other businesses in the community, which is a vital service essential for modern commerce. Banks make a profit by charging their depositors various fees for their services and by charging interest rates on the loans they make to their depositors. Additionally, banks make money by using depositors' money for investing and then pocketing the profits after they pay their depositors an advertised interest rate.

Bank Fees: Various fees charged by a financial institution. Common Fees:

- Checking Monthly Service Fee: Typically $10 to $15 a month. Sometimes you can avoid these fees by keeping a minimum balance or just asking for a fee-free checking account.
- ATM Fee: A fee charged if you use an ATM out of your banking ATM network. Learn which network your bank uses and always check before you use the ATM.
- Foreign Transaction Fees: Your ATM may (or may not) charge you a fee if you use an ATM in another country. Check with your banking institution.
- Account Closure Fee: If you open an account and then turn around and close it right away, usually within 90 days, the financial institutions charge a fee.

Bank Run: This was a common practice during periods when the economy had a downturn, and some banks were failing. When negative financial news about the bank was reported, depositors would flock to their bank and demand all their money to save their funds from being absorbed by a pending bank failure. The banks, who had the money invested, were unable to pay all the depositors at once, causing many bank failures. Creation of the *Federal Deposit Insurance Corporation* (FDIC) was the government's response. The FDIC now insures depositors. *See Federal Deposit Insurance Corporation.*

Bitcoin: The very first cryptocurrency invented by Satoshi Nakamoto. He proved the concept that blockchain technology works, which stemmed from a report he wrote on the subject. Nakamoto is an alias, and his real identity is still allegedly unknown, even after all this time and countless investigations. Bitcoins are not physical coins, but encrypted code on a network. The encrypted data protects a ledger type of sequential data blocks (called block chains/*see below*) that verify the code is real and allow tracking of the bitcoin's ownership history. Bitcoins are hidden on a decentralized network specifically designed to store Bitcoins.

Blockchain Technology: A coded ledger system that is kept within a decentralized network (much like the internet). Each blockchain is both coded and linked to all the other chains. The blocks form a ledger that follows a Bitcoin from the moment of inception to its present-day location. It is nearly impossible to hack into this type of system, as each block is coded, verified by the entire network, and linked by a code (in date order) to every other block—like a chain. This system is typically used for Bitcoin but can be used for virtually any ledger information that must be maintained tamper free or secret.

Board of Directors: A group of people elected by shareholders who oversee the business strategy of the corporation and assures management follows it. The board also elects the corporation's officers and decides if profits will be shared with investors or reinvested back into the business.

Bonds: Bonds are IOUs, or loans, issued by entities that require cash. Bonds can be issued by the federal, state, local government, or specially organized government entities like a transit authority or even foreign governments. Other classes of bonds can be issued by corporations and other businesses.

Bond Components:
- **Call Date:** The maturity date or the date the bond ends.
- **Coupon Rate:** A term for the interest rate a bond will pay
- **Par:** The face value of a bond or the amount of the loan
- **Bond Interest Rate:** The interest rate, or bond coupon rate, a bond pays is related to:
- **Federal Reserve Interest Rate** or **Prime Rate:** The rate banks charge to loan each other money to make up for FDIC-required cash on-hand.
- **Bond Term:** The length of time the bond issuer has your money. The longer a bond's term, the more interest that bond will pay you. The higher rate is compensation for tying up your money for a longer period.
- **Creditworthiness** (bond issuer): Those who are less creditworthy (meaning a greater risk) must pay more interest to those who loan them money in order to be able to sell

their bonds—no one would buy them otherwise. This is the same situation where you must pay more for a loan if you have a poor credit rating.

Bond Value: When the interest rate rises on newly issued bonds, old ones with lower interest rates become worth a little less in the resale market. After all, why would someone buy a bond with a lower interest when they can easily get a higher rate? Older bonds with lower interest rates can only be resold at a discount. This is relevant if you own a mutual fund that holds bonds. The value of your bond fund goes down if new bonds pay higher interest rates. Of course, if you buy the bond yourself, you may keep the bond until maturity and not lose money. Conversely, should interest rates fall, the bonds you own with a higher interest rate can suddenly become worth much more on the resale market.

Broker: *See Stockbroker and Brokerage Firm.*

Brokerage Firm: A government-licensed company that acts as a middleman to find, purchase, and sell investments for individual investors. Typically, fees/commissions are charged for buying and selling investments and the maintenance of client's (your) investing accounts. A firm will help you set up accounts and then provide you with opportunities to buy and sell various investments. Brokerage firms will also manage (buy/sell) your investments for you in exchange for an additional fee. They make the majority of their money by charging these fees (commissions) for their services. Brokerage firms will also set up retirement-focused accounts, such as IRAs, Roths or even a combination of all of them. You must have a basic knowledge of investing, so you understand what an advisor (sometimes called a stockbroker) is recommending and whether that investment is appropriate for your established goals.

Bubble: A rapid rise in an asset price that is not justified by the asset's returns. Eventually bubbles burst and prices fall significantly—sometimes to zero or next to zero. Bubbles are hard to spot when they are occurring and are usually only identified after that fact.

Budget: A budget is a spending plan for your income for a set period of time, such as a day, a week, a month, or even a year or more. Typically, households complete monthly and yearly budgets. In a budget, you analyze your anticipated income and then scrutinize all your anticipated expenses. The goal of personal budgeting is to use the information to both direct and control your spending with the objective of paying all your bills and then creating financial savings at the end of each budgeting period. A budget allows you to make decisions about how you will spend your money.

Budget Formula: Income - Fixed Expenses - Variable Expenses = Savings

Business Founder: *See Founders.*

Buy and Hold Strategy: An investment strategy where the investor buys an asset (usually stocks) and holds it long term (years to decades) despite short term up and downs in the market. The historical success of this strategy is very high and is preferred by famous investors such as Warren Buffet.

Buy Here, Pay Here Loans (for cars): A type of car loan offered by a car dealer that provides you with financing when you buy one of their vehicles. The financing is designed to maximize their profit from those with poor credit scores. Dealers take advantage of low credit score buyers by pricing their cars higher and charging a very high interest rate. A very aggressive repossession policy is written into the contract so the dealer can take the car back if the buyer falls behind on payments.

Cash Flow: The flow of cash being transferred in and out of your household bank accounts. Your cash flow should be positive, meaning you have enough cash inflow to cover all your bills (outflow of cash).

Certificates of Deposit (CD): Investment product similar to bonds offered by banks and credit unions. They borrow your money by selling you a CD and typically offer you a higher interest rate than a money market account or just a normal savings account, but lower than a longer-term bond. The term for CDs typically runs from six to eighteen months but can range from three months to years. Many banks and credit unions will let you automatically repurchase another CD at the end of your current CD's investment term.

Checking Account: An account at a bank or other financial institution where you can make deposits and withdrawals, typically used to pay your bills. Checking accounts were named after the paper-and-pen "checks" that direct payments from your checking account to a business or person. All checks are routed through the Federal Reserve's check clearing system, and it can take several days for the funds to transfer from your account to the entity being paid. Today, you can create instant electronic fund transfers (EFTs) from your checking account to those you want to pay using mobile payment applications and skip the old-school check writing almost entirely. Some banks will even charge you a monthly service fee for a check-writing account.

Collateral: An item of value you agree to forfeit to the lender if you don't pay your loan.

College Experience: Living outside parental control for the first time, which involves academic work and connecting with classmates who have similar interests.

Commodities: Physical goods such as wheat, rice, cooper, gold, oil and other items used in manufacturing and food processing. Various amounts of the commodity can be bought and sold, or contracts to provide these items in the future (called futures) can be bought and sold. Commodities are considered a hedge (protection) against inflation. When the cost of goods rise, so do the prices of commodities—usually. You can also buy stock or shares in a corporation that trades these goods on the open market with the goal of making a profit.

Common Stock: *See Stocks.*

Company: A legal enterprise formed to operate a business to make a profit.

Compounding Interest: Interest either paid to your various creditors (companies who loaned you money), or you can earn compounding interest on your various investments. Compounding interest occurs when a loan or an investment earns interest not only on the balance, but also on the interest accumulated (to date) each month. The next month, you earn interest on the even larger amount. If left alone and allowed to compound, the balance gets larger and larger (continues to compound) until it becomes a massive amount.

Confirmation Bias: A strong and harmful human tendency to only pay attention to information that confirms what we already believe and rejects information or narratives that challenge our beliefs. Confirmation bias usually leads to financial losses due to poor financial actions or purchases.

Corporation: *See Public and Private Corporations.*

Corporation's Officers: The board of directors appoints officers (senior executives) to run a corporation. Officer positions include jobs such as chief operating officer (COO), who is responsible for all day-to-day business and chief financial officer (CFO), who is responsible directly or indirectly for all the corporation's financial matters.

Cost of Goods Sold (COGS): Includes the costs of materials, manufacturing costs and labor costs required to produce an item for sale. This cost is typically subtracted from revenues to determine gross profit.

Credit Agencies: Government-sanctioned, private businesses (not actually official government bureaus). Your payment history along with all the information you completed when you filled out a credit application is provided to these credit agencies. Based on their research and the FICO scoring process (*see FICO*), these agencies produce reports about your creditworthiness, which are given to any potential creditors (people who are considering loaning you money) who request them.

Credit Card: A credit card is a pre-approved loan of a predetermined amount. You must pay back any of this borrowed money at a predetermined interest rate. You apply to various banks, credit unions and other lending institutions to get credit cards. They review your application and approve or deny you based upon your FICO score. You can use the card to access the funds made available to you. Some lenders charge an annual fee (in addition to interest) for the use of their credit cards.

Credit Score: A score that ranges from zero, meaning no score, up to a possible top score of 850. The higher the score, the less risk you pose to a lender to loan you money. Typically, those with a high credit score obtain a lower interest rate from creditors.

Credit Report: A report produced about your creditworthiness from credit bureaus, which is supplied to creditors who base their willingness to loan you money on the results of this report. The credit bureaus produce a FICO score that is published in their report on you.

Creditworthiness: The risk you represent to those who would loan you money

Crossover Point: The point where your investments pay you more than your wages pay you.

Custodial Account or Custodial Brokerage Account: An account for a minor that is managed by an adult, or an account set up and managed for the benefit of a future beneficiary.

Cryptocurrency or Crypto: An entirely digital currency (not physical coins) that is not government supported. Cryptocurrency transactions are both recorded and then verified by a decentralized network system using cryptography and blockchain technology. The currency is not issued by any centralized government agency. One of the supposed attractions with the blockchain system is that it allows only so many coins to be produced within its structural framework. Another attraction is that no bank or government is needed to complete online transfers (called peer-to-peer transactions).

Debit Card: A card attached to your checking account that is used to pay merchants and the money is withdrawn directly from your checking account for payment. The big selling point of debit cards is that they bypass the need for writing checks.

Defined-contribution Plans: Company retirement plans that are funded primarily by the employee. Companies will frequently (but not always) match employee contributions up to a certain percentage of the employee's pay, but it is up to each employee to fund their own plan.

Depositor: A customer of a financial institution (bank, credit union, etc), who keeps their money in the institution.

Direct Deposit: Your paycheck funds are electronically transferred straight to your bank/credit union using the Automated Clearing House (ACH) network. Your paycheck summary (stub) is routed to you via your employer. You can also designate the deposit of your funds each pay period to different accounts. For example, you can direct $300 from each paycheck to your savings account while the rest of your money is routed into your checking account.

Direct Expenses: The direct costs of goods and services you purchase.

Diversity: In the investing world, this means owning many different asset classes and different investments within those classes.

Dividends: Many larger corporations or companies will distribute some of the profits back to its owners, called shareholders (or stockholders), proportional to their corporation ownership (number of shares they own). The amount of each dividend (per share) is determined by the corporation's board of directors. Some companies traditionally pay dividends monthly, quarterly, semi-annually or annually while others reinvest the profits back into the corporation.

Dogecoin: A cryptocurrency created in 2013 as a joke between software engineers Billy Markus and Jackson Palmer. The joke was that this is "dog money," meaning that it is worthless. Elon Musk and others made it popular. Each digital coin (not a real coin) features the picture of a Shiba Inu (a breed of dog) from a famous dog meme where the dog is lying on the couch with a look of concern on its face, like it is watching a disaster unfold before it. It was initially used on the Reddit app between users for making funny comments.

Dollar-cost Averaging: A universally accepted investment strategy that involves buying a set amount of investments each month routed from your paycheck straight to your investment account, which helps even out the cost of your investments over time. For example, if you buy a certain amount of an index fund each month, this creates a situation where you end up buying more shares of the index fund when the market is down and less when it is higher. Over time, this has proven to be a successful strategy.

Earned Income Tax Credit: An example of a refundable income tax credit for low to moderate level income earners. If the credit exceeds your bill, the government will provide you with the remaining amount in a check or direct deposit into your account.

Electronic Communications Network (ECN): An electronic network that connects stock exchanges and matches buyers with sellers. Brokers also use this network to place and fill investment orders and investment sales.

Electronic Fund Transfers (EFT): An electronic or digital fund transfer from bank to bank. The transfer does not use bank employees but is done electronically at the time of the transaction.

Ethereum (ETH): A cryptocurrency called Ether, created in 2015 and designed by Vitalik Buterin and Gavin Wood and Joe Lubin (founder of blockchain software company ConsenSys) in 2015.

Exchange Traded Fund (ETF): An investment fund similar to a mutual fund that involves investors buying stocks so the fund's manager can invest in the fund's publicized strategy. Unlike mutual funds, however, shares in an ETF can be bought and sold all day long by stockbrokers, which means the price of a share is in constant flux.

Expenses: Goods and services requiring money to purchase. Some of these goods and services are essential to modern life, while other expenses are considered a luxury.

- **Monthly Fixed Expenses:** Expenses that will be the same every month, such as a car payment or rent
- **Monthly Variable Expenses:** Expenses that vary from month to month, like groceries or gas

Expense Ratio: The price (percentage of the money you're investing) you are charged for the fees associated with stocks being bought and sold and other direct expenses. Also, *see Management Fee or Administrative Fee.*

Federal Deposit Insurance Corporation (FDIC): The FDIC is an independent agency of the federal government established in 1933 that ensures your money up $250,000 per account against bank failures. Failures happen more often than you might think due to financial mismanagement or other problems.

Fee: A charge in exchange for a service.

Fair Isaac Corporation (FICO) Score: Your loan information is entered into a copyrighted computer formula and analyzed by the FICO software corporation. FICO scores are determined based upon your payment history, the amount you owe, length of your credit history and any new credit you may have taken out recently.

Financial Independence: Creating enough wealth that you no longer require a traditional job to support yourself (*also known in the text as prosperity*).

Founders (business): The people who invested the initial capital, took the risks and put forth the effort to create the business.

Futures: A future is a contract based on the anticipated future price of an investment like stocks and bonds or a commodity. People buy and sell futures in an attempt to make money through speculation and to offset possible losses should the price of an asset move in the wrong direction. Also, a process used by manufacturing or food producers to even out the costs of supplies or raw materials. For example, parties may write a contract to deliver a bushel of corn on a certain date at a specific price to a food processing plant. This contract can then be bought or sold in the open financial markets.

Gap Insurance: Auto insurance that will pay the difference between your car's value and the larger amount you still owe your lender for your vehicle should something happen to the vehicle, and it is totaled.

Generally Accepted Accounting Practices (GAAP): Accounting or bookkeeping practices that provide a high degree of transparency. These practices are recommended for small corporations or companies but are not required. For public corporations regulated by the SEC, however, these accounting practices are required along with a variety of reporting requirements.

Gross Pay: Total amount you are paid before taxes and various payroll deductions.

Hyperbolic Discounting: Choosing smaller immediate rewards instead of waiting for larger rewards in the future. It commonly leads to procrastination.

Income: Funds coming to you either through work or investments.

- **Income, Monthly:** The total amount of money you make each month
- **Income, Net:** Take-home or net pay. Your income minus all taxes and payroll deductions
- **Income stream:** When a corporation, a company or a person generates a steady inflow of money. In personal finance, multiple income streams are more desirable.

Income Tax: The fee that local, state and the federal government charge you to fund the government. Typically, the amount you pay is based on a percentage of your income. High earners pay a higher percentage of their income in taxes. Nearly all income is taxable. If taxes are not paid at the time your income is earned, they must be paid either quarterly or at the end of the year (depending on the amount).

Income Tax Deduction: Almost all income is subject to taxes. In some specific cases, the government has decided to grant an exception to specific income and specific uses of money to pay certain bills—like the money you donate to charity—meaning the money you utilize to pay that amount will not be counted as income and will be exempt from income taxes, assuming you complete the proper tax paperwork. The advantage is that this lowers your overall tax bill at the end of the year.

Index: A theoretical grouping of stocks that mirror a sector of our economy (*see below*).

Index Fund: A mutual fund or an exchange traded fund (ETF) that mirrors the index it reports to follow. It is considered a passive fund in that no manager is "actively" deciding which investments to buy and sell, which leads to low maintenance fees. Instead, they simply follow the index, making this the most purchased investment vehicle in history. Stock index funds and bond index funds can only be bought and sold at the end of the day. ETFs can be bought and sold throughout the day.

The most widely followed indexes in the U.S. are:
1. S&P 500: An index of America's 500 largest corporations. A large cap generally has a net worth of over 10 billion dollars.
2. Dow Jones Industrial Average (DJIA): Commonly called the "Dow." An index of 30 corporations that trade on the New York Stock Exchange. It is considered a barometer of how our economy is doing.
3. Nasdaq Composite: The "NASDAQ" is a grouping of large tech corporations.
4. Russell 2000 (RUT): This is a "small cap," index, meaning that each corporation has a value (capitalization) up to 2 billion dollars. The Russell 2000 tells us how small businesses are faring in the investment market and in our economy.
5. Wilshire 5000: Called the total market index, a selection of 5,000 stocks that represent small, mid-size and large corporations.

Indirect Expenses: The costs you pay for the depreciation or wear on items you previously purchased, such as the depreciation on your vehicle.

Individual Retirement Account (IRA): Unlike a 401K, you set up a traditional IRA with a brokerage firm and fund it entirely on your own without employer sponsorship or contributions. Again, all the money you invest will be considered tax deferred, grow tax free and only be taxed at your normal income tax rate when you begin removing the funds beginning at age 59 1/2. How much you contribute to a personal IRA is not impacted by you or your employer's contributions to your company's 401K plan. You may typically contribute up to $6,000 (2023) into this tax-deferred account.

Initial Public Offering (IPO): A private company's progression to a public corporation and its initial offering of stock shares to the investing public.

Interest Rate: The fee you pay on your loan for borrowing the lender's money. Or in investments, the fee you obtain for investing your money. For example, a 4% fee on a $100 loan would be an interest payment of $4.

Internal Revenue Service (IRS): A government agency established by Abraham Lincoln in 1862 under the U.S. Department of Treasury. The IRS is responsible for collecting taxes and enforcing tax laws related to citizens, companies, and corporations. The IRS also conducts criminal and fraud investigations.

Investing: A strategy to grow your money or create wealth. You buy assets that produce an income, increase in value, or both. The idea is to use your money to generate profit. If it is not expected to make a profit, then it is not investing.

Investing Diversity: An investing strategy where you own several different asset classes and several different investments within those different classes.

Investing Risk: *See Risk.*

IPO: *See Initial Public Offering.*

Investment Portfolio: *See Portfolio.*

Job: You provide labor and time to an employer. In return, you receive financial compensation or pay.

Labor: The utilization of your time, energy, effort, and intellect to accomplish your employer's goals.

Liability: The money you owe on your debts.

Litecoin: A cryptocurrency created in 2011 by Charles "Charlie" Lee, a former Google engineer. One of the primary features of Litecoin is that this blockchain system/software produces the coin and ledger system and more coins can be created than Bitcoin.

Loan: A sum of money that you borrow. Typically, you pay back the borrowed money, interest on that money, and any fees charged by the lender, which is the true cost of a loan.

Loan Fees: Costs you are or can be charged when taking out a loan.

- **Application Fee:** This is a fee charged to a potential borrower for processing and underwriting a loan application, which is required for nearly all types of loans.
- **Monthly Payment:** An amount based on the variables you agree to with the lender. You can get a rough estimate in advance based upon a car loan calculator or an amortization table.
- **Origination Fee:** This is an upfront fee that lenders charge for a new loan application. The fee is usually quoted as a percentage of the total loan and falls somewhere between 0.5% and 8% or more of the loan's total.
- **Principle:** The amount borrowed.
- **Processing Fee:** This is a fee for processing your loan paperwork. It can be a flat rate or it can be charged per transaction.
- **Term:** Length of loan.
- **Total Interest Paid:** The amount of interest paid over the life of the loan. This number is typically provided by a loan calculator or an amortization table.

Loan Amortization Table: A table or chart of anticipated loan payments once the variables (like interest rate) are considered. The table lists the number of payments, payment amounts, total interest paid and total amount paid on the loan.

Management or Administrative Fee: The fee you are charged for having a professional stockbroker manage your investments. This charge covers the salaries and bonuses and other personnel related costs to manage the fund (*see Expense Ratio*).

Mobile Payment App: An easy-to-use, digital application that creates an instant EFT (Electronic Fund Transfer) from bank to bank. Typically, you initiate a transfer from your smartphone or other mobile device. Money is transferred from your bank account you previously linked to your mobile application to whomever you have chosen to receive your funds. Payment applications can be linked to a credit card or debit card. Unique codes are generated by each transaction, so the person being paid does not have your banking or credit card information. Mobile payment apps are super-convenient and very safe. Most payment applications will charge you a fee if your payment is linked to your credit card (usually 3% to offset the fee they must pay the credit card company for every purchase). Typically, you will be charged no fees if your payment app is linked to a bank account, and you don't require immediate deposit. The most commonly used mobile payment applications are:

- **PayPal:** If linked to a credit card rather than a bank account, it charges both the payer and the merchant 3% with each transaction.
- **Venmo:** The app typically used to send friends or family money. You can split restaurant bills or transfer money to family or friends with this app and leave them a message along with the money.
- **Cash App:** Links to your bank account via a debit card. You can also buy and sell Bitcoin with this app.
- **Zelle:** This app supports mobile banking as well as the transfer of money from your bank account to someone else's. Currently, it is favored by credit unions and many large banks.

Mutual fund: A type of holding/investment corporation that buys and sells shares (stocks or other investments) in a professionally managed fund that has a publicized investment strategy. If interested, investors buy shares of that mutual fund. A professional manager hired by the fund buys stocks, bonds, real-estate and other investments to pursue the investing strategy for its shareholders.

National Credit Union Administration (NCUA): Manages the National Credit Union Share Insurance Fund (NCUSIF), which is insurance on your savings and checking accounts at credit unions. The NCUA insures these accounts at the same level as FDIC.

Needs: Essential bills that you must pay each month, including items such as housing, utilities, transportation, etc. (*see Budget*).

Net Asset Value (NAV): In this book, it refers to the total assets of a mutual fund, minus its liabilities and its relationship to the price someone must pay to buy into the fund.

Net Pay: Your paycheck minus monthly taxes and other payroll deductions, also known as your take-home pay.

Net Worth: All your assets minus all liabilities.

Non-Fungible Token (NFT): The term non-fungible means you can't trade it for a like or similar item. NFTs use blockchain technology to create original, digital art. Although art can always be copied, the blockchain code will easily distinguish the original from any copies that are produced. NFTs typically take the form of a picture, meme, GIF, game token in a video game or even a digital baseball card.

Non-refundable Income Tax Credit: A tax credit (the actual amount in dollars) that can be deducted from your annual tax bill. An example would be the child or dependent care tax credit. If the tax credit is more than your tax bill, you will not be paid the excess in a refund check.

Non-sufficient Fund Fees (NSF Fee): If a bank notices you have insufficient funds in your account and declines a transaction before it goes through, you will still be charged a fee (NSF fee).

Online Banks: These types of financial institutions provide convenient, 24-hour access from your mobile device with the same FDIC protection as a brick-and-mortar commercial bank. You can electronically deposit checks and pay bills right from your phone or computer. The fees are usually less than traditional brick-and-mortar banks because online banks are not maintaining physical branches. They also typically have lower interest rates loans. Online banks have the normal savings and checking accounts.

Overdraft Fee: If the bank fails to notice you have insufficient funds in your account and the transaction goes through, you will be charged an overdraft fee for spending more in your account than is available (*see Non-sufficient Funds Fee*).

Payday Loans: A loan typically used by those who have a limited ability to obtain credit due to poor credit scores or by those who don't know they can easily get better deals. These loans have an interest rate of 28% or higher, which would be illegal in other situations. Lenders also usually have a very aggressive collection policy.

Payroll Deductions: Money taken from your payday check for healthcare, company saving/investing plan, vision, dental, taxes, Social Security payment, etc.

Penalty Fees: If you are late with a loan payment, you can be penalized through late fees, overdue fines and even charged processing fees for your late payments. Avoid these fees by paying bills on time or early.

Portfolio or Investment Portfolio: A collection or basket of different types and classes of assets such as stocks, bonds, mutual funds, real estate and many other investments held in an investment account or accounts.

Preferred Stock: *See Stocks.*

Prepayment Fee: A fee you are charged should you decide to pay your loan off early. This assures the lender they will make a certain amount of money on you. Again, this loan is their asset, so they want to assure they will make a certain percentage from your loan.

Pre-tax funds: Gross pay (before taxes) or any money you receive for which you have not paid taxes.

Principle: An amount invested in any particular investment.

Private Corporations: The majority of corporations are organized under state law—usually to protect the owner from civil livability—and have not gone "public", which has many regulations attached to the designation. Private corporations have more freedom from federal government regulations. Shares or ownership of private corporations are sold privately and are not available on a stock exchange (*see Public Corporations*).

Prospectus: A required legal document released by a corporation producing the investment (such as a mutual fund, a corporation releasing stock or some other investment) that explains the investment and includes an investment's financial details, its management and the strategy being pursued. If a corporation is releasing stocks, for example, it will explain how the corporation is organized, its market share, its competitors, and any other relevant information to help an investor make a decision about purchasing the investment. The prospectus also lists all the fees paid by the investor. The prospectus is known to the average investor as being a long, legalese-filled document that is hard to read and understand.

Psychological Momentum (PM): A positive self-perception that improves behavior and allows one to perform at an increased level of achievement.

Public Corporation: A company that has become its own "legal person" through legal filings and has the right to take out loans and enter into contracts entirely independent of its owners. This protects the owners from liability. A public corporation must also have shares of stock available for sale on the open market or a stock exchange. Public corporations are also required to follow Generally Accepted Accounting Practices (GAAP) and file quarterly and annual reports, income statements and a host of other reports. Public corporations are regulated by the Securities and Exchange Commission (SEC).

Quarterly Report: A report the SEC requires public corporations to file every three months. The report contains the public corporation's income statement (profit and loss over the last quarter), cash flow (inflow and outflow of cash) and a balance sheet (list of assets and liabilities).

Real Estate Investment Trust (REIT): Investors pool their resources (money) and form a corporation that purchases and maintains income-producing, commercial real estate. REITs typically dispense profits by paying dividends to its shareholders (via stocks). The REIT manages all the needed investment purchases, sales and maintains all the properties it owns. By purchasing a REIT, you need no maintenance or real estate knowledge to potentially profit from the real estate market. Owning a REIT fund is a way to participate in real estate value gains and the income streams these properties can produce. I much prefer owning REIT shares compared to owning actual real estate with the never-ending maintenance requirements.

Refundable Income Tax Credit: A tax credit (amount paid in actual dollars) that can be deducted from your annual tax bill. If the credit is more than your bill, the government will provide the remainder of your tax credit in a refund check or direct deposit.

Return On Investment (ROI): A gauge to determine if an investment is profitable. The rate of return is generally expressed in a percentage, which is the net profit minus the cost of the investment.

Risk: With respect to investors, the degree of probability that your investments will suffer a loss or economic downturn, including a total loss of your principle (the amount you invested). For stock investors, two basic types of risk exist:

1. Systematic risk has to do with a downturn in our economy and generally drags nearly all stocks/corporations lower in value—at least temporarily. Stock owners will see the value of their companies sink lower.

2. Non-systematic risk is when a company or a particular industry does poorly because of changing economic conditions, incorrect strategies or a poorly run corporation. In such a situation, your stock's value could even drop to zero.

Roth Individual Retirement Account (Roth IRA): A Roth utilizes after-tax money you receive in your paycheck. You pay all normal income taxes on the income you use to fund your Roth. You may withdraw the money you contributed (principal) at any time (after five years) without taxes or penalty, but you must leave the Roth profits in the account until you are fifty-nine and a half. At that age, all withdrawals are completely tax free. You can contribute up to $6,000 annually (with certain annual income limits). In most cases, you may only contribute a total of $6,000 between your traditional IRA and your Roth IRA. Contribution limits are typically increased annually.

Savings Account: Unlike a checking account where money is constantly flowing in and out, you deposit your money into a savings account to keep it secure for a longer period yet still have easy access to the funds for emergencies. You are usually paid a small amount of interest on the money kept in your savings account, but some banks may charge you a service fee for frequent withdrawals.

Securities and Exchange Commission (SEC): The securities and exchange commission is a federal government agency charged with investigating securities or investing fraud. Essentially, you alone are responsible for researching and investing your money responsibly. In cases where you were defrauded of money or sold something you were told had value when it had no value or did not exist, the SEC may investigate for possible criminal offenses. The government's goal, however, is prosecution and not necessarily the return of your funds.

Shared Branching System: A national network of credit unions, which enables you to walk into any participating shared branching credit union and route your deposit to your account at your own credit union, make a withdrawal or pay funds to a third party.

Shareholder: An owner of company shares (stocks) in a public corporation, also known as a stockholder.

Speculation: Guessing about future events and their impact on the prices of investments in an attempt to make a profit.

Stellar Lumens (Lumens): A cryptocurrency created in 2014 by Jed McCaleb in an attempt to help people overcome the problem of cross-border payments. The coin is called a lumen.

Stock(s): The ownership of a portion (or share) of a corporation that entitles the owner to a share in the profits/losses and assets of the corporation equal to their proportion of ownership. Stocks range from risky (the corporation may go broke) to secure (less risk). Two types of stocks:

1. **Common stock:** represents ownership and gives the

owner a voting right in how the corporation is run and maintained.

2. **Preferred stocks:** do not allow voting privileges, but the owners receive dividends (cash payments) based on the corporation's profits before any common stockholders. If the company is dissolved, they also get first shot at the company's assets.

Stockbroker: An advisor from a brokerage firm who advises you on which investments to buy or sell and then helps you execute your investment strategy for a fee. *See Brokerage Firm.*

Stock Exchange: Used interchangeably with the stock market, it is an entity where stocks and other investments are bought and sold. Exchanges are worldwide and connected electronically. Only by using an authorized stockbroker can you access this exchange system.

Stockholder: A person who owns stock in a corporation. Stock is a share of corporate ownership.

Stock Market: *See Stock Exchange.*

Take-home Pay: Your paycheck minus monthly taxes and other payroll deductions, also known as your net pay.

Tax Deferred Account: An account that you pay no taxes on the money until you withdraw it. You pay the income tax rate on the money you withdraw that is relevant to your tax situation at the time of withdraw.

Tax Favored Accounts: *See Tax Deferred Account.*

Totaled: When an accident creates so much damage to an automobile that the money needed to repair it would cost more than the value of the vehicle.

Traditional IRA: *See IRA.*

IPO Underwriter: A financial institution that assists a corporation in determining share pricing, purchases unsold shares (typically at a discount), and then sells these shares to potential shareholders in an attempt to make a profit.

Upside Down: When the loan on your automobile exceeds the value of the vehicle. Being upside down on a loan typically occurs when you make a low down payment on a long-term loan to finance the vehicle. This situation could also occur if you rolled the balance you still owed on your previous vehicle into your new automobile's loan.

Volatility: In the financial world, sharp swings up and down in the price of an asset, usually measured by changes in the standard deviation of the price.

Wages: The amount your employer pays you based on an hourly or annual calculation.

Wants: In a budget, goods and services you want to buy or activities you'd like to do that are optional (like going out with friends).

Recommended Reading for Further Winning

Escape Debt Prison by Larry Faulkner and Lisa Faulkner

The Illustrated Guide to Financial Independence by Larry Faulkner

From Money Disaster to Prosperity: The Breakthrough Formula by Larry Faulkner and Michelle Bohls

Messages From Your Future: The Seven Rules for Financial, Personal and Professional Success by Larry Faulkner

The Index Card: Why Personal Finance Doesn't Have to Be Complicated by Helaine Olen and Harold Pollack

All Your Worth: The Ultimate Lifetime Money Plan by Elizabeth Warren and Amelia Warren Tyagi

Personal Finance for Dummies by Eric Tyson

Asset Allocation for Dummies by Jerry Miccolis and Dorianne Perrucci

Get Rich Slowly blog: getrichslowly.org

Rich Dad, Poor Dad by Robert Kiyosaki

The Automatic Millionaire by David Bach

A Random Walk Down Wall Street by Burton Malkiel

The Bogleheads' Guide to Investing by Taylor Larimore, Mel Lindauer and Michael LeBoeuf

Millionaire Teacher by Andrew Hallam

All About Asset Allocation by Richard Ferri

Index

Chapter 1 Citations:

[1] Carnegie, Dale. 1964. How to Win Friends and Influence People. New York: Simon and Schuster.

[2] Porter, Sylvia. 1976. Sylvia Porter's Money Book: How to Earn It, Spend It, Save It, Invest It, Borrow It, and Use It Better in Your Life. New York: The Hearst Corporation.

[3] https://www.psychologytoday.com/us/blog/dont-delay/200806/goal-progress-and-happiness

[4] https://www.ncbi.nlm.nih.gov/pmc/articles/PMC5006010/

Chapter 2 Citations:

[1] https://www.financialeducatorscouncil.org/vince-shorb/

[2] https://www.harvardbusiness.org/what-makes-storytelling-so-effective-for-learning/

[3] https://www.jumpstart.org/what-we-do/support-financial-education/reality-check/

[4] https://www.financialeducatorscouncil.org/national-financial-literacy-test/

[5] https://www.debt.com/news/teaching-kids-about-money/

[6] https://www.bizchair.com/about.html

[7] https://www.pnas.org/doi/10.1073/pnas.2016976118

[8] https://www.forbes.com/advisor/retirement/seniors-debt-statistics/

[9] https://www.inc.com/ilya-pozin/why-many-students-with-bad-grades-end-up-successful.html

[10] https://www.businessinsider.com/personal-finance/how-to-develop-traits-that-build-wealth-get-rich-2019-5

[11] https://news.fullerton.edu/2022/10/danny-trejo-reveals-secret-to-success-its-all-about-helping-people/

Chapter 3 Citations:

[1] https://medium.com/wharton-fintech/nfl-star-penn-professor-brandon-copeland-tackling-financial-education-through-life-101-9482e4d461b8

[2] https://www.moneycrashers.com/greatest-financial-regrets-older-americans/

[3] https://www.reuters.com/business/finance/americans-top-financial-regret-not-saving-an-emergency-2021-05-12/

[4] https://www.cnbc.com/select/73-percent-of-americans-rank-finances-as-the-number-one-stress-in-life/

[5] https://www.lendingtree.com/student/americans-wish-they-did-more-with-money-past-year-survey/

[6] https://www.usatoday.com/story/money/personalfinance/2017/10/06/why-half-of-americans-cant-come-up-with-400-in-an-emergency/106216294/

[7] https://www.fool.com/the-ascent/research/study-psychological-cost-debt/

[8] https://www.debt.org/advice/emotional-effects/

[9] https://www.magnifymoney.com/blog/investing/investing-regrets/

[10] https://www.businessinsider.com/millennials-regret-student-loan-debt-2020-1

[11] Ibid. businessinsider.regret-student-loan-debt, 2020.

[12] https://www.credible.com/blog/refinance-student-loans/ how-much-will-you-actually-pay-for-a-30k-student-loan/

[13] https://www.credible.com/blog/statistics/ average-time-to-repay-student-loans-statistics/

[14] https://www.debt.com/credit-card-debt/ how-long-to-pay-off-credit-card-balance/

[15] https://www.businessinsider.com/ millennials-regret-student-loan-debt-2020-1

[16] Ibid.businessinsider.regret-student-loan-debt, 2020.

[17] https://www.studentloanplanner.com/ student-loan-debt-statistics-average-student-loan-debt/

[18] https://www.wral.com/fact-check-how-many-student-loan-borrowers-failed-to-finish-college/19524091/

[19] https://fortunly.com/statistics/personal-finance-statistics/#gref

[20] https://www.aplu.org/our-work/4-policy-and-advocacy/ publicuvalues/student-debt/

[21] https://admin.insomniacookies.com/about

[22] https://www.fundkite.com/blog/insomnia-cookies-the-brilliance-of-marketing-towards-college-students/

Chapter 4 Citations:

[1] https://shiftprocessing.com/american-debt/

[2] https://www.thebalance.com/ biggest-budgeting-mistakes-2385610

[3] https://www.cnbc.com/video/2019/09/29/how-professional-gamer-jake-lyon-invests-and-saves-his-salary.html

Chapter 5 Citations:

[1] https://discover.hubpages.com/art/ grandma-moses-secrets-of-success

[2] https://www.businessinsider.com/
how-millionaires-build-wealth-consistency-2019-1
[3] https://www.businessinsider.com/
daymond-john-shares-his-daily-productivity-ritual-2016-2
[4] https://www.cnbc.com/2020/03/10/daymond-john-on-how-to-set-and-use-goals-to-achieve-success.html
[5] https://link.springer.com/article/10.1007/s10902-016-9750-0
[6] https://www.nfhs.org/articles/talent-vs-attitude/

Chapter 6 Citations:

[1] https://www.businessinsider.com/squid-game-reflects-reality-south-korean-household-debt-charts-2021-11
[2] https://www.cnbc.com/2022/03/03/60percent-of-teens-want-to-launch-businesses-instead-of-working-regular-jobs.html
[3] https://hbr.org/2020/08/
can-entrepreneurship-be-taught-in-a-classroom
[4] https://www.sciencedaily.com/releases/2007/05/070521152452.htm
[5] https://www.gsb.stanford.edu/insights/
focus-small-steps-first-then-shift-larger-goal
[6] Faulkner, Larry & Michelle Bohls. (2021). *From Money Disaster to Prosperity: The Breakthrough Formula.* Faulkner Financial Freedom. https://www.amazon.com/dp/B09J1L655S
[7] https://www.irs.gov/forms-pubs/about-form-1040-ez

Chapter 7 Citations:

[1] https://www.inc.com/amanda-abella/want-to-become-a-million-aire-create-multiple-streams-of-income.html
[2] Ibid. Inc. Want to Become A Millionaire. 2017.
[3] https://www.cnbc.com/2022/05/12/

how-this-29-year-old-built-a-million-dollar-business-after-getting-rejected-from-15-medical-schools.html

Chapter 8 Citations:
[1] https://www.zdnet.com/finance/banking/bye-bye-megabank-more-young-adults-are-adopting-digital-banking-to-manage-their-money/
[2] https://www.verywellmind.com/why-are-people-bad-at-long-term-planning-5225017

Chapter 9 Citations:
[1] https://www.thecut.com/2017/05/the-annoying-psychology-of-why-you-cant-stick-to-a-budget.html
[2] https://www.cnbc.com/2020/02/11/32-percent-of-workers-run-out-of-cash-before-payday.html
[3] https://womenwhomoney.com/inspiring-money-stories-skipping-degree/
[4] https://awmcap.com/podcast/nfl-20
[5] https://newsroom.ucla.edu/magazine/sense-of-purpose-happy-healthy
[6] https://www.cnbc.com/2017/11/21/harvard-researchers-say-a-purpose-leads-to-longer-healthier-life.html
[7] https://www.believeinmind.com/self-growth/famous-people-with-a-growth-mindset/

Chapter 10 Citations:
[1] https://www.forbes.com/sites/forbesfinancecouncil/2021/09/21/your-retirement-shot-clock-is-ticking/?sh=44c196ffa255
[2] Warren, Elizabeth, Amelia Warren-Tyagi. *All Your Worth: The Ultimate Lifetime MoneyPlan.* New York: Free Press A Division of

Simon and Schuster, Inc., 2005. Ebook Edition. Chapter 1.

³ https://mrjamiegriffin.com/my-first-budget-changed-my-life/

Chapter 11 Citations:
¹ https://www.nerdwallet.com/article/finance/
getting-out-of-debt-stories
² Faulkner, Larry. Messages From Your Future: The Seven
Rules for Financial, Personal and Professional Success. Dayton:
Faulkner Integrated Tactics, 2016. 13-30.
³ https://www.aspeninstitute.org/blog-posts/
real-stories-of-unmanageable-debt/
⁴ https://www.investopedia.com/personal-finance/
most-common-financial-mistakes/
⁵ https://www.bankrate.com/personal-finance/debt/
average-american-debt/
⁶ https://bit.ly/35zR5Rg
⁷ https://www.khou.com/article/money/magnify-money/8-inspi-
rational-stories-of-people-who-overcame-debt/507-537577067
⁸ https://educationdata.org/average-cost-of-college
⁹ https://www.foxbusiness.com/features/
skilled-labor-workforce-severe-nationwide-shortage
¹⁰ https://www.coursera.org/
¹¹ https://www.apprenticeship.gov
¹² www.bls.gov/oes/current/oes_nat.htm
¹³ https://www.indiatimes.com/trending/human-interest/ra-
mesh-babu-indias-billionaire-barber-548219.html
¹⁴ https://www.businessinsider.com/for-profit-colleges-al-
leged-fraud-student-loans-debt-cancelation-education-2021-3
¹⁵ https://www.ed.gov/accreditation

Chapter 12 Citations:

[1] https://www.quotespedia.org/authors/s/sean-patrick-flanery/do-something-today-that-your-future-self-will-thank-you-for-sean-patrick-flanery/

[2] https://www.irs.gov/newsroom/understand-how-to-report-large-cash-transactions

[3] https://bestcompany.com/credit-repair/blog/3-credit-repair-success-stories-and-tips-that-will-inspire-you

Chapter 13 Citations:

[1] https://www.thefinancialfreedomproject.com/compound-interest-part-5-benjamin-franklins-200-year-experiment/

[2] https://www.cnbc.com/2018/08/28/richard-branson-launched-his-first-business-for-less-than-2000.html

[3] https://www.cnbc.com/2017/11/13/branson-set-up-a-school-magazine-at-14-coke-and-pepsi-advertised.html

[4] https://www.investopedia.com/best-small-business-loans-5079093

Chapter 14 Citations:

[1] https://www.cnbc.com/select/why-retirement-saving-is-hard-according-to-behavioral-economics/

[2] Ibid.cnbc

[3] Ibid.cnbc

[4] https://www.cnbc.com/2019/09/04/the-age-when-americans-start-saving-for-retirement.html

[5] https://www.aarp.org/money/credit-loans-debt/info-2019/recent-grads-delay-saving.html

[6] https://www.futurity.org/money-confidence-2544162/

[7] https://www.ncbi.nlm.nih.gov/pmc/articles/PMC7542307/

[8] https://www.facebook.com/omgvoice/photos/a.260134164038742/3658687520850039/?type=3

Chapter 15 Citations:
[1] https://www.investor.gov/financial-tools-calculators/calculators/compound-interest-calculator

Chapter 16 Citations:
[1] https://topresultsacademy.com/authors/brian-tracy/biography/
[2] https://money.cnn.com/2015/04/28/investing/millennial-investor-17-year-old-brandon-fleisher/
[3] https://tradeciety.com/24-statistics-why-most-traders-lose-money/
[4] http://faculty.haas.berkeley.edu/odean/papers/day%20traders/Day%20Trading%20and%20Learning%20110217.pdf
[5] https://www.usbank.com/investing/financial-perspectives/investing-insights/buy-and-hold-long-term-investment-strategies.html

Chapter 17 Citations:
[1] https://www.cnbc.com/2021/05/27/this-millennial-couple-retired-in-their-30s-with-870k.html
[2] https://www.acorns.com/learn/retiring/personal-finance-tips-to-get-you-to-early-retirement/
[3] https://intelligent.schwab.com/article/determine-your-risk-tolerance-level
[4] https://www.fool.com/the-ascent/personal-finance/articles/this-couple-became-millionaires-in-10-years-heres-how-you-could-do-the-same/

Chapter 18 Citations:

[1] https://www.yahoo.com/now/10-famous-cryptocurrency-quotes-learn-180037674.html?guccounter=1&guce_referrer=aHR0cHM6Ly93d3cuZ29vZ2xlLmNvbS8&guce_referrer_sig=AQAAAHb1iOp_kcNaxu6dbtQdNgS4tCVIluyP196TU-TySo4irPNwl30giayw2FsyV7Tu0qf4yefWPKCAQj4gJY93U-CREXFwpT-qrwbg-4UDeyRoDuKV-a2olpN6igwmPIIhk-zR-P8lbVWba8aciFHGvNGaOyfuibFITioWJqTeIEcYpO7

[2] https://www.businessinsider.com/personal-finance/what-is-blockchain

[3] Interview with Torres on March 18, 2023, at 3:00 PM via the Messenger App.

[4] https://www.forbes.com/sites/eriksherman/2022/03/11/dol-has-big-worries-about-crypto-in-retirement-accounts/?sh=17b-c6a691e80

[5] https://www.businessinsider.com/who-is-erik-finman-bitcoin-investor-millionaire-2019-8#finman-grew-up-in-post-falls-a-small-town-outside-of-coeur-dalene-idaho-2

[6] FaulknerFinancialFreedom.com

[7] https://www.hollywoodreporter.com/business/digital/long-neckie-ladies-nft-artist-nyla-hayes-signs-with-caa-exclusive-1235102487/

Chapter 19 Citations:

[1] https://www.sidehustlenation.com/side-hustle-statistics/

[2] https://www.cnbc.com/2022/12/26/this-29-year-olds-side-hustle-brings-in-2-million-a-year-i-work-4-hours-a-week.html

[3] https://optinmonster.com/online-shopping-statistics/

[4] https://www.sidehustlenation.com/sneaker-flipping-reselling-shoes/

[5] https://brandbuildersgroup.com/podcast/ep-140-how-to-get-millions-of-followers-on-tiktok-with-maggie-thurmon/

[6] https://influencermarketinghub.com/tiktok-highest-paid-stars/#toc-3

[7] https://www.popbuzz.com/internet/viral/bella-poarch/navy-army/

[8] https://www.faulknerfinancialfreedom.com/

Chapter 20 Citations:

[1] https://www.investopedia.com/news/number-millionaires-continues-increase/

[2] https://spendmenot.com/blog/what-percentage-of-americans-are-millionaires/

About Larry Faulkner

Larry Faulkner is a self-made millionaire, an award-winning author, and a certified financial education instructor.

He decided he wanted to be a millionaire in high school, but several years and two divorces later, Larry saw his dream slipping away. He was deeply in debt and barely scraping by each month.

Larry recommitted to his goals and began educating himself on budgeting, saving and investing. When he met his wife, Lisa, they realized they shared a vision of financial independence, so they worked together to achieve their dream.

A former officer for the Dayton, Ohio Police Department, Larry began teaching other officers what he had learned. This led Larry to obtain his certification as a financial education instructor. He then began teaching financial literacy classes for his fellow officers, fire-fighters, public safety personnel, and even doctors.

Larry and Lisa have designed and taught financial wellness classes to public and private entities to promote financial awareness and literacy to workers—typically as a community service. Larry and Lisa also designed and taught a special multi-week financial rebuilding class to prison inmates, to give them the knowledge they need to financially rebuild their lives after release.

Larry is the author of numerous best-selling and award-winning books. Despite numerous invites to do so, Larry never sells investments or financial products to anyone. Instead, he spends his time and energy educating people on the advantages of financial literacy and how such knowledge can enrich your life.

Made in the USA
Las Vegas, NV
08 January 2024

84095537R00182